Purple Scribbles

AND THE PLAN FOR YOUR LIFE

Purple Scribbles

AND THE PLAN FOR YOUR LIFE

VIRGINIA DAWKINS

XULON PRESS

Xulon Press
2301 Lucien Way #415
Maitland, FL 32751
407.339.4217
www.xulonpress.com

ISBN-13: 978-1-6628-5539-9

Table of Contents

Introduction

We have become His poetry, a re-created people that will fulfill the destiny He has given each of us, for we are joined to Jesus, the Anointed One. Even before we were born, God planned in advance our destiny and the good works we would do to fulfill it! –Ephesians 2:10, Passion Bible

What if God's plan for His world was like a great big jigsaw puzzle with millions of pieces, and when the time was up for completing the picture and the available pieces were in place, there could be seen many little open spaces spoiling the beauty of what could have been a beautiful picture. Could it be that each person born into the world has a place in God's big picture? Could it be that many of us leave gaping holes in God's plan because we never find our place in the world?

How can we find our purpose? Is it possible that we can each take hold of our gifts, sharpen them, and fit ourselves in between other pieces of the puzzle to become a part of the Big Picture?

In *Chasing Vines,* Beth Moore tells us: "We all want to matter. Such a longing is sewn in permanent thread within the fabric of every human soul. Let the Maker show you why you matter... We were created to contribute."

Referring to God's instructions to Moses in the Old Testament, Mark Batterson writes in *The Grave Robber*: "The Architect of the universe laid out every square inch of the tabernacle so there was a place for everything and everything was in its place. With that same type of intentionality, God plans our plotline. He orders our footsteps. He prepares good works in advance. And He works all things together for good. God has given us free will, but no one orchestrates opportunities like the Omnipotent One. He provides an entry ramp into every opportunity."

"Your very hands have held me and made me who I am."
–Psalm 119:73 Passion Bible

Chapter One

Providence

Before I formed you in the womb, I knew you...
—Jeremiah 1:5

You formed my innermost being, shaping my delicate inside and my intricate outside, and wove them all together in my mother's womb... How thoroughly you know me, Lord! You even formed every bone in my body when you created me in the secret place, carefully, skill-fully shaping me from nothing to something. You saw who You created me to be before I came to be me. Before I'd even seen the light of day, the number of days you planned for me were already recorded in your book.
–Psalm 139 Passion

PURPLE SCRIBBLES

You aren't an accident. You weren't mass-produced. You aren't an assembly-line product. You were deliberately

planned, specifically gifted, and lovingly positioned on
earth by the Master Craftsman.

–Max Lucado

I walked up the tall steps of Oakland Heights Elementary School, inhaling a mixture of scents, waxy crayons, oily floors, and chalk dust. I entered my first-grade classroom clutching the little draw-string bag my mom had sewed. It held my new collection of treasures: a jar of paste, a pair of blunt scissors, and a brand-new box of jumbo crayons. This was the day I had waited for; I was finally old enough to be in a real classroom with a teacher, a blackboard, and stacks of books.

I slid into my desk, reached into my bag for a plump, purple crayon, opened my Red Chief tablet, and began making marks across the fresh page. The red-haired teacher appeared tall above me with a frown on her face, and that's when I stopped creating my purple picture and began watching my classmates. When I compared my scribbles to their drawings, I understood why the teacher was frowning. I let go of my crayon and let it drop to the bottom of my little bag. At that moment, I was sure something was wrong with me, and I was determined to watch closely at what the others were doing and try harder to be like them.

Weeks later, my teacher continued to frown as she whispered to my mom, "Mary Virginia is a slow learner." I heard that whisper and felt those words plaster across my forehead.

Nevertheless, something wonderful happened that year—I received my first book. I found myself peeping through new wire-framed glasses at a colorful little book with bold black letters under each picture. Just holding that little book in my hands made me happy, and very soon, I heard words coming from my own lips: "Run, Spot, run! Look, Jane! See Spot run." I had learned to read!

I don't remember other books or events from the second through fourth grades, but I'll never forget my fifth year. When I walked into Mrs. Flossie Shackleford's classroom, she stooped down and smiled straight into my eyes, as if she did not notice the words scrawled across my forehead. She led me into the enchanting world of story, as she announced to the class: "After recess, I'll read you another chapter of *Little Women*." It was like offering me ice cream and cake in the middle of the day. I could rest my head on the desk as Mrs. Shackelford read words that painted pictures in my mind.

At ten years old, I had no idea that God had a plan for my life, or that my life even mattered in this world. But Mrs. Shackelford knew her place in the world. She gave value to my life and opened doors to places I had not known.

I would not hear until I was middle-aged the description my Uncle Nelson gave of me as a little child. He said, "I would watch you play— you were just a little rolling ball of promise." Now I know that even when I was making purple scribbles on my Red Chief Tablet, God had plans for me.

> *There are no worthless people, just people who have been misfiled, mis-appropriated, misallocated, those who need to be reassigned to the purpose for which they were created.*
>
> *It is when we consult God that He directs us into His divine purpose and we establish together a plan that is much like prebuilding."*
>
> —Author Unknown

THE MAKING OF AN ARTIST

Providence: *I believe in a Sovereign God who is ordering your footsteps, preparing good works in advance, and making all things work together for good.*
> —Mark Batterson

Pat Kent was meant to be an artist. I see so clearly God's Providence in her life. He planned it before she was born giving her the gifts and abilities she would need, a family who encouraged her and placing her in a city where her gifts could be nurtured.

Pat told me that when she was a little girl she was fascinated with the templates, pencils, and the quill pens her father, a draftsman, used in his work. He kept his tools in leather cases with velvet linings; often at the end of a workday, he would encourage his little girl to reach inside and pull out those implements to make her own markings. "And Mother was a doodler," recalls Pat, she absentmindedly drew faces in the margins of newspapers or on paper napkins while talking to her friends on the phone." In this environment, doodle drawing became a daily activity for the small child. Pat also remembers taking great delight in practicing her strokes in Penmanship class while many of her classmates considered the process boring.

Pat is a native of New Orleans and began her study of art in the New Orleans Public School system. Later, she attended the famous John McCrady Art School in the French Quarter. She has pleasant memories of strolling through the Quarter, feasting on the sights—the rich architecture of the buildings and the quaint courtyards. Such fare was nourishing food for a budding artist's eye.

Pat believes that her talent began as a gift from God. Her mantra is that of an ancient Danish proverb: "Creativity is God's gift to me. Using and developing this gift is my gift to God." Thus, Pat works at her craft with persistence, and she continues to enhance her skills by attending workshops where she studies under nationally acclaimed artists. Her work has appeared in numerous art exhibits, from Mississippi to Colorado.

"Potentiality thrives on encouragement," says Pat, "I remember a special moment in Beauregard Junior High, when a teacher commented on my work. I can see it now—a fall scene with pumpkins. My teacher liked it, and though I don't remember her exact words when she walked away, I was infused with new energy." Pat also remembers an instructor who discouraged her when he said, "You'll never make a living at this!" She explains that although she has sold many paintings through the years, it is not the money that gives her satisfaction. "It's the process of painting that gives me pleasure," says Pat. "There's nothing like receiving feedback from those who enjoy my interpretation of God's creation—now that gives me pure joy."

Nevertheless, Pat tells me there are enemies to her creativity. She experiences non-productive days when her well seems dry. In those times, negative thoughts dominate her mind, she has doubts about her ability and finds it hard to focus. However, she has discovered a way of refilling the creative well by focusing away from herself and concentrating on her faith. "If I could plan a perfect day to rejuvenate my thoughts," she says, "I would spend relaxing hours in the gazebo underneath the pine trees in my own backyard. I would read from the Bible, spend time in prayer, and meditate on God's handiwork in the trees and flowers around me. I could then go into my studio and paint with new energy."

Travel seems to be another way of stirring up creative juices for Pat. When she and her husband travel out west to visit their children, she takes her paints and a sketchbook to capture scenes along the way. She considers the Grand Canyon one of God's most amazing creations; she loves the abstract lines and the colors that only God could mix. She says, "God's ever-changing universe never ceases to challenge my artistic eye, and it is with a reverence that I attempt to interpret the wonders of this earth. The beauty of the earth is God's gift to all of us."

Patricia Kent believes that it all began when God dropped the gift into her spirit, and she believes the Master Designer then whispered: "Now go to work and use well what I have given you."

A GARDEN, A LIFE

A garden is only yours as long as you seed, weed, cultivate, water, and prune. A garden needs lots of tender, loving care. It's lots of work, softening the soil with hoeing and fertilizing, planting, and watering. Protect the seed from vermin. Prune when things grow too fast and wild. The

5

whole point, don't you see? Bearing fruit and carrying the
sweet aroma.

–Francine Rivers, *Leota's Garden*

On sunny, spring days, garden stores are overflowing with ladies poking around among bedding plants and planning their gardens. I'm not much of a gardener, but I'm right there with those ladies, buying seeds and soil for my zinnia beds.

I'm always inspired by other people's gardens. I'm thinking of a yard in an older neighborhood, where a profusion of color peeps out through a white, picket fence. The unique personality of this garden derives from the owner's careful arrangement of healthy plants inter-mingled with quaint, one-of-a-kind objects. I don't think the gardener preplanned the décor, but it developed as she collected things that called to her—a sale on bedding plants, a display of hand-crafted birdhouses at a flea market, and a collection of hand-painted feeders. The thing that holds it all together is the work the gardener continually puts into her space—planting, watering, feeding, seeding, and protecting her plants from vermin.

How like a garden is a life. Each life is different. Some are well-tended and skillfully grown. Some are mediocre and plain, and others are scraggly and neglected. Some thrive and grow and bear good fruit.

Solomon, a great horticulturist, assures us in Proverbs: "He who cul-tivates his garden will have plenty of bread." It sounds like God is saying: Look and see the raw material I've placed in your care. If you do your work, you'll have everything you need. You'll begin to bear fruit right there in your particular space, and you'll have enough to share with a hungry world.

Paul instructs us to "Live creatively... Make a careful exploration of who you are and the work you have been given and sink yourself into that. Don't compare yourself with others. Each of you must take respon-sibility for doing the creative best you can with you own life" (Galatians 6:1-5 Message Bible).

It's hard work making the most of your life. It's not always fun when you're digging. Maybe you pray for sun and it wilts your plants. You wake up one morning and something invisible seems to have invaded and drained the life out of the petunias. That's when you look over the fence at what the neighbors have and wonder what's wrong with you.

Nevertheless, one morning there's a tiny, green sprout peeping out of the soil and you know that God is still in control of growing things in your garden. So, if you will keep watering and weeding and trusting Him, something will grow and bloom and bear good fruit.

The seasons pass quickly and all too soon the flowers fade. But even in the dead of winter, there are holly bushes and pansies that thrive in snow. If you've worked your garden the best you can, then after you've left this earth, something you planted will remain to bless others.

PAINTING YOUR LIFE

If you hear a voice within you say you cannot paint, then by all means paint and that voice will be silenced.
–Vincent Van Gogh

He was called "The Painter of Light," painting pictures of quaint English cottages and stately Victorian houses with lights in every window. In his time, it was estimated that one in every twenty American homes owned a copy of Thomas Kinkade's work. He authored ten books, including the story of his childhood which was made into a movie, "The Christmas Cottage." When he died at fifty-four, he left behind a legacy of beautiful treasures—paintings, books, and encouraging ideas.

Kinkade believed that art has the power to touch hearts and change people's lives. He said, "I paint to benefit and enrich the life experiences of others, creating pictures that encourage people and bring them a sense of peace and joy. I want to inspire them to catch a vision of a better life." He was criticized by other artists for making his art prints affordable for middle class families.

In his book, *Light Posts for Living,* he affirmed his basic values of faith in God, home, family, and the joy of a simpler way of living. It was his belief that, "Your life can be a beautifully crafted work of art. With every moment that you experience, every choice you make, you are adding brushstrokes to your canvas. And each life has the ability to touch other lives."

Although "Light" was his trademark, he confessed that if people came into his studio while he was beginning a painting, they were often surprised and disappointed to find his work-in-progress to be quite dark and gloomy. This was because he deliberately painted layer after layer of dark glaze across his canvas as a first step. He considered the dark layers a necessary preparation for the luminous colors he would add later. There is a chapter in *Light Posts* called "The Secret of the Dark Canvas," in which he explains: "Those dark layers are what will give my work its depth. They will make the windows and the streetlights and even the sun to glow from within instead of being dabbed on the surface." Similarly, he believed that, "The dark times in my own life—the neglect of my alcoholic father and the constant struggle to help my mother provide for our impoverished family, added depth to my own character."

Kinkade believed that what was true in his own life was also true in the lives of those who read his books and bought his paintings. He believed that despite our circumstances and human failings we each have a God-given purpose for being on this earth. He said, "Your life really is part of an unfolding plan, a charted voyage, and an exquisitely executed work of art. Every circumstance in your life, every event that occurs is moving you a little closer to your final destination. Every response you make adds another brushstroke to the final picture."

Leaving a legacy of exquisite art and amazing words, sadly, Thomas Kinkade's final brushstrokes upon his own life seem to have shortened his life. Nevertheless, his gifts remain in our homes today, the houses with lighted windows are on our walls and his books are in our shelves to be read again and again.

THE PURSUIT OF HAPPINESS

Life is a struggle and the potential for failure is ever-present, but those who live in fear of failure, or hardship, or embarrassment will never achieve their potential. Without pushing your limits, without occasionally sliding down the rope headfirst, without daring greatly, you will never know what is truly possible in your life.

–Admiral McRaven, *Make Your Bed*

"I made a solemn promise to myself," said Christopher Gardner, "that when I grew up and had a son of my own, he would always know who I was and I would never disappear from his life. I was never going to terrorize, threaten, harm, or abuse a woman or child and I was never going to drink so hard that I couldn't account for my actions." This was his declaration after many years of not knowing who his father was, of suffering abuse from an alcoholic step-father, and living in extreme poverty.

However, in the midst of a troubled childhood, there were encouragements for the young boy. His mom would say, "Chris, if you want to, one day you could make a million dollars." She would also instruct him, "The public library is the most dangerous place in the world because you can go in there and figure out how to do anything if you can read." She admonished, "Boy, it's better to have a degree from God and self-knowledge."

Uncle Henry was also an encourager, trying to pass on everything he had seen and learned in his life. He would say, "Here it is, Chris, the world is your oyster. It's up to you to find the pearls." He told Chris to become a voracious reader of books, to pursue a vision, and live large.

When Chris grew up and became a father, he experienced true happiness for the first time. He would say, "This must be what heaven is like. I was here in this time and place, being with this beautiful little boy. The idea occurred to me that this was something that was supposed to be passed down from generation to generation, fathers playing ball with their sons and sitting side by side to look at books together. It just hadn't happened when I was a son."

And then one day, Chris became a single father with no one to help raise his child. He lost his job and became homeless. He and his little boy spent many nights in homeless shelters. Sometimes when the shelters were full, they would have to lock themselves inside a public restroom for the night. Chris began to wonder, "Maybe we can only pursue happiness and never really have it."

Every Sunday morning, he prayed to find his way out of the problems. "Reverend Cecil Williams was my mentor," said Chris. "He fed, housed, and repaired souls at the homeless shelter. His advice was, 'Walk the walk and go forward all the time. Even baby steps count.'"

With his little boy in hand, he continued to walk the walk and go forward. As he struggled with what seemed to be baby steps, doors opened and he would begin to use the unique gifts and abilities that were God-given. His success story was made into a movie, and he says, "The movie, *The Pursuit of Happiness,* is the story of my life, but it's not about me. It's about anybody who ever dreamed big and had someone tell them, 'No, you can't do it. You can!'"

FROM UNDER THE BRIDGE

Remember, who you are going to one day be, you are now becoming. Don't wait. Start today. now is the time for you to become the best version of yourself—the one that was intended for you from the very beginning.
                                        –Andy Andrews

When we are busy making foolish mistakes and unable to see our way forward, God still has a place for us in this world. This is the message Andy Andrews often shares in his writings.

For one year, Andrews was homeless, sleeping under a bridge or occasionally in someone's empty garage. The downhill slope began when he lost his mother to cancer and his father died in an automobile accident. Following these tragedies, the nineteen-year-old made a series of bad choices which led him to take shelter many nights under the Gulf State Park Pier on the Alabama coast.

Sitting under the bridge, he pondered this question: "Is life just a lottery ticket or are there choices one can make to direct his future?" In search of wisdom, he haunted the public library, eventually reading more than 200 biographies of great men and women. From the lives of such famous people as Harry Truman, Cristopher Columbus, Anne Frank, Abraham Lincoln, and biblical characters like King Solomon, he found a common thread; each made a handful of decisions that determined their ultimate success.

Today, Andy Andrews is a Best-Selling novelist and an in-demand speaker for some of the world's largest organizations. He has spoken at the request of four different United States Presidents. A New York Times reporter said of Andrews, "He is someone who has quietly become one of the most influential people in America."

THE PURPOSE OF TODAY

We have to believe that where we were yesterday and where we find ourselves today matter for who we become tomorrow.

–Joanna Gaines

It seems that God's plans for his children seldom follow a smooth, straight path; there are often sharp curves, washed-out bridges, and detours to experience before one's life-purpose is accomplished. We don't always see the purpose of what is going on in our lives at the present moment in relation to the grand purpose of our being.

Joanna struggled with doubts about her future. She worked in her father's tire shop, and then earned a degree in journalism; receiving a journalism internship, she went alone to live in New York City. "It was my first time living away from home," says Joanna. "So, in addition to being a nervous wreck, I was realizing that the world of television news wasn't meant for me. Most days, I'd leave my internship feeling uncertain or just plain homesick." The best part of each day became her walk home when a creative window display or the familiar scent of a lit candle would lure her inside one of the cozy shops that lined the city streets. She didn't know that God would use her shop wandering later on. There was another "best part" of her New York stint, it was during her homesick time in the big city that Joanna began seeking God.

Leaving New York, she returned to work in her father's tire shop in Waco, where time moved in slow motion. "I watched as friends moved on and into careers while my own life felt like a piece of luggage left behind on an airport conveyor belt, going round and round, waiting to be picked up for its grand adventure." She questioned, "What is the purpose of my life?"

Later, she met and married Chip Gaines. They toured New England on their honeymoon, returned home broke, and lay down to sleep on the floor of an 800-square foot house with stinky carpet and no electricity. Eventually, they would restore, decorate, sell that little house, and repeat this process with numerous houses. By this time, both Joanna and Chip began relying more on their faith in God and listening to His whispers for direction. Sometimes they seemed to misunderstand God's direction and made mistakes. But Joanna would often say, "God has not brought us this far to let us down now." Soon HGTV would offer them a reality show—Fixer Upper.

Today, they are flipping houses and cooking on their own television network. Chip and Joanna have published books that have been on bestseller lists. They produce a popular magazine, *Magnolia Journal,* and their most valued accomplishments are their five children.

Now, they look back and see that there was a purpose for each season of their lives. Chip and Joanna both agree that, "The dream isn't about fame and fortune. For us, the dream is that we get to wake up every morning and do what we love with the ones we love.

LINDA'S WILLING HEART

What small things can I do today to bring a blessing to someone else?

—Light Posts for Living

"Finding your life's purpose can often feel just out of reach," writes Joanna Gaines in *Magnolia Journal Magazine,* "a maybe someday' revelation you hope to discover. But what if your purpose is already circling your feet—and the very things you are meant to breathe life into are actually, remarkably, within reach? What if your purpose comes from entirely unplanned circumstances, and suddenly, what you are meant to do is simply to respond with a full heart?" Can you say to yourself, "I am here for such a time as this?"

Linda followed her grandmother into a little church, and there she found God. He had always been near, but now she could feel His presence and He became more real to her than ever before. Now that she was a born-again child of God, she wondered what she could do for the Lord. She began to look around in the little church and found that bathrooms needed to be cleaned. So, she cleaned the bathrooms. The wooden pews needed dusting; she dusted, and as she did, she prayed, asking God to bring in her family members to sit in those pews.

Eventually, she was asked to teach children. Although she had no experience in teaching, she began leading Children's Church. She bought herself a clown suit and became Clooney the Clown; the children loved it! Later, her pastor opened a radio station and asked Linda to conduct a daily radio program where people called in with prayer requests. This made her a little nervous, but she did it. Mothers and grandmothers often called, asking Linda to pray for their prodigal children. She prayed, and God answered those prayers.

She had always wanted to play the piano, so she asked someone who had a musician's gift to pray for her. He did, and she began playing the piano and singing praise songs. Eventually, Linda became an anointed praise and worship leader.

Throughout her born-again life, my friend Linda has paid attention to those things circling her feet and she has always responded with a trusting heart. What is lying at your feet? What do you already have in your hand? What are the needs where you are standing? That's where you begin, and the Lord will take it from there.

THE WIFE OF NOBLE CHARACTER

Her husband is known in the gates, where he sits among the elders of the land... Strength and honor are her clothing.... She opens her mouth with wisdom, and on her tongue is the wisdom of kindness. She watches over the ways of her household, and does not eat the bread of idleness. Her children rise up and call her blessed; her husband also, and he praises her.

—Proverbs 31

I know a lady, who knew from a very young age her life's purpose. Her awareness of God began when she was a child sitting in the swing with her grandfather—while swinging back and forth, they would sing hymns together and praise the Lord. Later, when she was fifteen, she walked down the aisle of her church and prayed a prayer that changed her life. "The Holy Spirit was speaking to my heart," says Joy, "He told me I needed Jesus in my heart. I said yes to Jesus, He forgave my sins, and I began to pray about everything." She talked to God about the desires of her heart, and one of her requests was to find a godly husband. A couple of years later she enrolled in college, and walking through the campus one day, a shy young man walked by her and smiled. When she returned the smile, the Lord whispered, "That's him, the one for whom you have been praying."

Soon after that, friends told her that Jack Giles already had a girl-friend and that the girlfriend was currently wearing his class ring. "Well, I was not about to get involved in that situation," says Joy. "My Father God would have to take care of that." Nevertheless, six months later, Jack had his ring back and he and Joy began dating. Joy advises, "If you leave everything in God's hands, He can work things out better than you can. You just have to be obedient to everything He tells you to do."

With her marriage, Joy knew for sure what God's purpose was for her life. She found her job description in Proverbs 31. When her husband chose to preach the Gospel, she vowed to be his helpmate, to stand beside him, and to support his ministry.

During seasons of earnest prayer, Pastor Jack received messages from the Lord. One such time, he received the distinct word that he and Joy should sell their house, and with the money from the sale, begin building a Christian school. He was not sure how he would tell his wife of this conviction. But he didn't worry long, because Joy confessed to him that the Lord had given her the very same message. With no regrets, Joy and Pastor Jack gave up their comfortable home and lived in a small mobile home for four and a half years. Eventually, the Christian school was built, and then, God gave the Giles a much nicer house than the one they had given away.

Through the years, Pastor Jack Giles' unique ministry has reached far beyond his own church. Recently, I read a description of Mother Teresa that reminds me of my pastor: "She walked the streets of her city to visit the sick and needy. Along the way, she will search for those cast aside by the rushing world: the sick, the unstable, and the unwanted. She will touch each one intentionally, so that they will know the Love of Christ."

I wonder how that once shy young man could have touched so many lives with the love of Christ without a Proverbs 31 helpmate. The Giles' ministry has been a partnership, and I believe that when the two of them reach heaven, many voices will greet them saying, "Thank You for giving to the Lord, for I am a life that was saved."

MR. ROGERS

When I was a boy and I would see scary things on the news, my mother would say to me, 'Look for the helpers. You will always find people who are helping.' To this day, especially in time of "disaster," I remember my mother's words, and I am always comforted by realizing that there are still so many helpers—so many caring people in this world.

–Fred "Mr." Rogers

Kindness and empathetic outreach had motivated Fred Rogers since he was a sickly, chubby boy himself. His classmates called him "Fat Freddie" and chased him home from school. While being chased by bullies, Fred often found protection in the homes of people in his own neighborhood. Instead of playing outside with other children, the lonely, only child often spent school lunch breaks in his puppet theater in the attic of his parent's home. These humble beginnings, the bullies, the friendly rescuing neighbors, and time spent in the puppet theater, all worked together to bring forth an American icon. Every weekday, for decades, a kind man named Mister Rogers stepped through a door of his TV house, spoke directly into the camera, and sang, "It's a Beautiful Day in the Neighborhood." The soft-spoken icon became a household name for tens of millions of children.

For almost forty years, as the creator and star of public television's "Mr. Rogers' Neighborhood," Fred Rogers was a champion of compassion, equality, and kindness. Because his childhood had often been a scary world, his mom told him to look for the helpers, because there were many kind and helpful people in the world. Fred Rogers became one of those kind, helpful people.

To Rogers, every child required special attention, because every child needed assurance that he or she was someone who mattered. Week after week, as children watched the show, he would look into the camera and say, "It's you I like. I like you just the way you are."

Viewers and those who worked with Rogers agreed that Mr. Rogers' Neighborhood was full of wonderful values with issues that affected families. Rogers and his puppets spoke to children about their fears, their joys, apprehensions, and those things they did not understand.

In *The Good Neighbor*, written by Maxwell King, the story is told of an autistic child and his family who visited the "*Neighborhood*" set. When Fred came out to visit with the family, he had King and Queen puppets on his hands. He talked with each member of the family, and when he came to the autistic child who had never spoken before, the boy began speaking in full sentences to the King and Queen puppets. When the father heard his son speak for the first time, he began to cry.

Fred Rogers read his Bible daily and endeavored to live by its principles. When he walked into the studio each day, he said a silent prayer, "Dear Lord, let some word of this be yours."

QUAKER MINISTER ELIZABETH FRY

When Elizabeth Fry visited Newgate Prison in London, England, in 1813, she found half-naked women and their children struggling together, with the most boisterous violence. She said "I felt I was going into a den of wild beasts." However, Mrs. Fry did nothing sophisticated in order to initiate reform but began reading her Bible to the prisoners. Soon, a great change occurred, and an observer described the scene: "There they sat in respectful silence, every eye fixed upon the gentle lady, never till then, and never since then have I heard anyone read as Elizabeth read."

Elizabeth Fry was the driving force in English Prison reform, and her work was supported by the reigning monarch, Queen Victoria. Fry inspired other women to play fuller roles in society, for in these times, it was unusual for women to be involved outside the home. She was a staunch Quaker who believed that old people, including criminals, were children of God and deserved fair treatment and reformative efforts, not punishment alone. She believed that love was the greatest gift one could give to the poor, the sick, and the imprisoned.

She encouraged women: "If you will do what you can do, God will do what you cannot do. Then doors will open, and a way will be made, and creative ideas will come." She said, "Inspire others—each person doing a little, together we can make a big difference."

SUSANNA WESLEY

I pondered how a person's life causes ripples in others' lives in ways and at times that person could hardly imagine.
—Susanna Wesley

Susanna Wesley, born in seventeenth-century England, endured a mother's greatest sorrow with the loss of nine of her nineteen children who died at birth or were born sickly and died young. She lived an impoverished life and endured frequent illnesses while living with a husband who nurtured his own dreams over those of his family. The family experienced political upheaval, their house was burned to the ground on a cold winter night, and baby John nearly lost his life in the fire.

Susanna had grown up envying her brothers who were allowed to go away to college, in a time when women were not afforded that privilege. She educated herself by constantly reading books from her father's library. Although her choices were limited, she was determined to walk in the light she was given each day, always obeying the commandments of God. She believed she would achieve this by ordering her days, by rising at the same hour each day, eating meals, and having prayer and devotions at the appointed hour.

Years later, Susanna would homeschool her children, ordering their days in a methodical fashion. She would see that each child would study six hours a day. As soon as each could speak, he or she would memorize *The Lord's Prayer.* They were assigned a chapter of the Old Testament for morning readings, and a chapter of the New Testament in the evening.

As the years went by, the older children would help teach the younger ones. Each child would spend one hour each week in private conversation with their mom, where Susanna would get to know each intimately, talking with them about their fears, their hopes, and dreams.

While women were ordered to keep silent in church, Susanna taught the Bible to large groups of people in her home. She also tutored and nurtured impoverished, unwed mothers, when the church was neglecting them

Through hardship and bouts of depression, she would continue walking in the light she was given each day, all the while making holy ripples in the lives of her children. John and Charles Wesley grew up, went away to college, and began making holy ripples throughout England and across the ocean to America. It was said that Susanna Wesley's sons turned England upside down for their Lord and Savior Jesus Christ.

Chapter Two

Facing the Giants

———⋘❦⋙———

Between you and your goal will be a series of obstacles.
                                    –John Maxwell

History has demonstrated that the most notable winners usually encounter heartbreaking obstacles before they triumphed. They won because they refused to become discouraged by their defeats.
                                    –B.C. Forbes

TRAMP FOR THE LORD

My life is but a weaving, between my God and me.
I do not choose the colors, He worketh steadily.
Ofttimes, He weaves sorrow, and I in foolish pride,
Forgetting He sees the upper, and I the underside.
Not till the loom is silent and shuttles cease to fly,
Will God unroll the canvas and explain the reason why.
The dark threads are as needful in the skillful weaver's hand,
as the threads of gold and silver in the pattern He has planned.
                                    –Corrie Ten Boom

In Holland, the foreshadowing came with a rock through the window of a Jewish-owned store, an ugly word scrawled on the wall of a synagogue, or a sign in a shop window stating: "Jews will not be served here." Very soon a library, restaurants, theaters, and synagogues, were burned down. Firetrucks came, but only to keep the flames from spreading. Under Hitler's regime, Germany was systematically teaching disrespect for old age and contempt for human life. The old, the weak, and those who disagreed with government policy were to be eliminated. Soon, Jewish families were disappearing from the streets.

"One day, as Father and I were returning from our walk," said Corrie, "we found the Grote Market cordoned off by a double ring of police and soldiers. A truck was parked in front of the fish mart; into the back were climbing men, women, and children, all wearing the yellow star. There was no reason we could see why this particular place at this particular time had been chosen." In shock, Corrie cried, "Father! Those poor people!"

Corrie, her sister Betsie, and their father had often talked about what they could do to help their Jewish friends. Eventually, Corrie and her family risked their lives to help Jews and underground workers escape from the Nazis. The Holocaust would soon take the lives of Corrie's family members. Corrie would suffer from the horrors of the prison camps, but would miraculously survive and live to proclaim the miracles of the Lord.

She said, "The world is my classroom. The school of life offers some difficult courses, but it is in the difficult class that one learns the most—especially when your teacher is Jesus Himself. Looking back across the years of my life, I can see the working of a divine pattern which is the way of God with His children."

DYSLEXIA

Those who knew Albert Einstein as a child described him as mentally slow, unsociable, and dreamy. His sister reported that he spoke very few words until he was seven years old. Today some believe he was a dyslexic genius.

The term "dyslexia" describes a learning disability that often causes one to reverse letters or numbers when reading. It can affect reading, writing, spelling, and pronouncing words. This can be especially confusing to a child. Best-selling author Debbie Macomber recalls:

"I was the only girl in my first-grade class to be in the Robin Reading Group, the lowest level there was. My teacher told my mother that I would never do well in school." Debbie remained a very average student in grade school; her spelling was atrocious, and she could never achieve good grades in English. Her teachers described her as an aimless dreamer. This happened in the fifties when no one had heard the word Dyslexia.

Despite her learning disability, Debbie dreamed of becoming a writer. After many years of determined faith and hard work, Debbie Macomber became a New York Times best-selling author. More than 140 million copies of her books are in print; they have been translated into twenty-three languages, and some have been made into Hallmark movies.

Debbie explains that the dyslexia has never gone away. She says, "To this very day I'm a slow, thoughtful reader and a 'creative' speller." Nevertheless, she is absolutely convinced that each of us is created with a God-given purpose and that God's purpose for her was to become a writer.

Bodie Thoene also had difficulty learning to read. When she was in third grade her Sunday school teacher demanded that she stand and read the words of a song in class. When she could not, her teacher ridiculed her in front of the other students. Bodie ran out of the class in tears, and then she began to pray. "Hello up there, I am Bodie. I ran away from Sunday School. I'm sorry. I can't read the songs. I don't want to go back to Sunday school until I can read. I want to read like the other kids." She made a bargain with God: if He would teach her to read, she would write something and read it just for Him.

Eventually, due to faith, prayer, and persistent work, Bodie and her husband Brock published over forty-five works of historical fiction, sold more than ten million copies of their books, and won eight Gold Medallion awards.

THE WOUNDED SPIRIT

They pick on you because you are smaller, because you wear a particular sweater, you can't throw or catch a ball, you can't run fast, you don't have the right clothes, because you pick apples on the way home from school, or because you sing a different song.

—Frank Peretti, *The Wounded Spirit*

Frank Peretti was marked with disfiguring birth-defects and walked funny when he was a little boy. Even in kindergarten, he felt ugly, rejected, and picked on. He ran away from school when he was in first grade, but his parents made him return. The bullying accelerated to a new height in junior high where he was shoved, insulted, badgered, manhandled, teased, and harassed. There was nowhere to run. "They were constantly stabbing me with words, kicking me, hurting me, and taking away my dignity," says Peretti. "And if you reported the bullying you endured, you were a snitch or a wimp. At least that seemed to be the universal, unwritten code of conduct."

When Peretti wrote *The Wounded Spirit* in 1999, he was close to fifty years of age, but he still remembered the names and faces of those individuals who had made his life a living hell. He remembered their taunts, their blows, their spittle, and the humiliations.

"I remember the thoughts I had, sitting alone on the street curb, eyes watering after P.B. sprayed deodorant in my face," says Peretti. "I remember what I wished I could do if only I had the strength and the skill in martial arts. But my parents taught me that I had a loving God to turn to when times were tough." Peretti believes that having a Christian home with loving parents who prayed saved him from retaliating in some violent way against his enemies.

Frank Peretti survived the bullying and grew up to become a best-selling author. The abuse he suffered at the hands of the bullies actually prepared him to write books that help and inspire people today.

LIVING IN A NON-HEARING WORLD

Our niece's husband, Scott, became deaf when he was a small child. He grew up in a non-hearing world, developing a healthy sense of humor about his life. He can hear certain sounds but has difficulty under-standing words. However, he is an excellent lip-reader, and I enjoy face-to-face conversations with him and the stories he tells. Scott posted this story on Facebook:

> "Years ago, when they started the drive-thru restau-rants, you drove up to one window, gave your order to a person, paid, then drove to the second window to pick up. No problem, I could handle that. But then they added the speakers and there were no lips to read. That's when the problems started. I would drive up, hear a voice with a six-syllable staccato, and assume they were saying, 'Good day, may I help you?' Then I would make it simple like, 'Number 7 with a medium sweet tea.' I would repeat it twice, and then after all the gibberish coming from the speakers, I'd say, 'That's right. Thank you. Bye.'

> With many attempts, I learned to anticipate the ques-tions they were asking, like, 'Do you want Crispy or Grilled chicken?' Well, not long ago, tired, hungry, and needing a late lunch, I pulled up to the speaker and asked for a Chick-fil-A sandwich and an unsweetened

tea. After which, a lot of gibberish came through the speakers—more than usual it seemed. I had no idea what was going on. So, twice I said, 'That's right. Thank you. Bye.' I then drove up to the window, and the person there told me to repeat my order again. So, I did. And then she tells me, 'This is McDonald's. 'Chick-fil-A is across the street!' Well, that's my life."

When Scott was a young boy, there were times when other kids played tricks on him. He remembers a time when he went with some friends to explore a cave. When the boys reached the deepest part of the cavern, one of them suggested they turn off their flashlights just to see how dark it really was. When all flashlights were switched off, someone suddenly grabbed Scott's flashlight, and according to plan, each boy moved out of Scott's reach. He describes a moment of panic when darkness and deafness overpowered him. At first, he screamed and tried to reach for a human hand. There was none. His panic subsided as he remembered that God is in dark places too. That's when he sat down and waited quietly. Finally, out of curiosity, each of the pranksters clicked on their flashlights.

Scott and his wife Becky live in Virginia, not too far from Washington D.C. When my husband and I visited them, Scott insisted that we go to the Kennedy Center to hear the Washington Symphony Orchestra. He secured seats in the third row, right in front of the violins. It was wonderful. Afterward, when Scott remarked that he also had enjoyed the performance, we asked, "But Scott, could you hear any of the music?" He answered, "No. but I saw the amazing precision of the instruments. All those violinists moved together like one hand and one violin. It was amazing—a beautiful symphony!"

Recently, Scott retired as owner and operator of a very successful commercial landscaping company. He writes:

"Yesterday, I signed the agreements to sell my company. I am officially retired after thirty-six years, eleven months, and four days of the greatest adventure of my life. This wasn't the only occupation I had during my career. I worked in research, first in microbiology, studying viruses and bacteria. This included working with those scary Rhesus monkeys with their three-inch fangs. I even worked in the lab building where the infamous Ebola virus outbreak occurred. I then moved to another company doing research as one of the eleven pioneers researching in what we thought was a cure for cancer but ended up becoming the flagship product of biotech giant, Biogen, for treating MS.

From there, I went on to literature research in chemical carcinogens and teratogens, including publishing books as a technical writer, then editor. None of those occupations suited me. Out of desperation to be free, I started a commercial landscape company in 1985. Other than marrying my wife, it was the best decision I ever made. It was the ultimate wild thrill ride with many stories enriching my life and forming lasting bonds with employees who became friends and family.

Being a Christian and also a maverick, I chose to be different. We never used a website and only hired a salesperson for one year, but we always had more work than we could handle. I give God the glory for all the business we received.

Being deaf since childhood, I have never talked on the phone, yet God brought incredible people to work for me and miraculously grew the company rapidly and exponentially, sometimes defying logic. Even during the selling process, I could see God's hand at work. We had the largest landscape company in the country.

So, a chapter of my life ends and the next one begins. I don't know what this next chapter will be like, but based on all the incredible things I have experienced so far, it's going to be another exciting adventure."

ELIZABETH SMART

History is replete with stories of human suffering. I am not the first one to suffer. But the human spirit is resilient. God made us so. He gave us the ability to forgive and to look forward instead of back.

–Elizabeth Smart

Elizabeth Smart was barely fourteen years old when she was abducted. She was forced out of her bed in the middle of the night. A knife was held to her throat, and she heard these commanding words: "Do what I say or I will kill you and your family." The knife, long and sharp, was pressing at her spine as the evil man forced her to walk up the side of a mountain to a filthy campsite where she would be chained like an ill-treated animal. For the next nine months, she would suffer pain, starvation, slavery, and horrible sexual abuse.

Nevertheless, Elizabeth believes she is alive today because God was with her and never left her side. She doesn't question the fairness of this horrible time in her life, and she says: "Being taken was not a part of some great, eternal plan of God, but an evil plan concocted by a man possessed by evil." Yet, in the midst of the evil darkness created by Brian David Mitchell, there were little flickers of light, miracles that could not be explained by natural reasoning.

One such miracle happened after three long days in the dry Utah desert, when temperatures reached above a hundred degrees, and there was no water. "My skin was dry, my throat, my eyes," Elizabeth writes. "I was dirty and so thirsty I thought I would die." In the middle of the night, as she lay on a mat inside the tent, she woke suddenly. She observed Mitchell and his wife Barzee sleeping soundly nearby. Then she saw a yellow cup beside her pillow that was cold as ice and filled to the top with water. "I picked it up and drank the water," says Elizabeth. "It was cold and clear and wonderful, the best-tasting water that I had ever had."

There was no natural explanation as to how the cup got there. There was no water beside her sleeping captors. She is convinced that it was a gift from God, reminding her that He was aware of her suffering and that He had a plan. She says, "God wanted me to know that He controlled the earth and all the heavens and that all things were in His hands."

Today Elizabeth Smart Gilmour is a nationally recognized advocate for children's rights. She helped promote the National Amber Alert and helped to develop a survivors' guide titled "You're Not Alone: The Journey from Abduction to Empowerment," to encourage children who have gone through similar experiences.

"I think there are far more miracles in our lives than we may ever realize," says Elizabeth. "Like flickers of light among the darkness, they remind us that God is there and that He cares."

HIGHER IS WAITING

Ever since I was a little boy, I've known there was something greater than myself: something bigger, something stronger, something higher.

–Tyler Perry

Today he is a writer, a filmmaker, a songwriter, and a philanthropist. Yet once, he was a shy little boy, growing up in New Orleans, suffering abuse from an alcoholic father. His memoir, *Higher is Waiting,* is about his relationship with the Creator God, the Savior, in the worst and the best of times. "My childhood was a story of discouragement, belittlement, and unthinkable abuse. What would have happened if not for two special women who brought sunlight into the dark, hopeless, places of my life? There was Mamma Maxine and Aunt Mae."

Conversations between Perry and his two favorite women would go like this:

"What are you doing, Aunt Mae?"

"Talking to Jesus, baby."

"How can you do that?"

"Well, did you say your prayers last night?"

"Yes, Mam."

"Then you were talking to Jesus."

Riding across Lake Pontchartrain, the little boy would ask, "Why doesn't the water cover the bridge?" Aunt Mae's answer was, "Because God's got it. He's in control. God is good!"

It seemed to the little boy that Jesus made Mamma Maxine and Aunt Mae happy in spite of trouble. When Tyler would ask, "What is faith, Mamma?" Mamma would answer, "Baby, faith is what you believe when you can't see."

When Tyler was older, he moved to Atlanta, in search of a better life. He says, "At first, living in Atlanta was a life and death struggle. I wanted to die." When he couldn't pay the rent, he became homeless and lived in his car. It seemed that he could no longer hear God's voice—something was badly wrong in his life.

Perhaps it was the ongoing prayers of those two special women that pulled him through. He would eventually remember Aunt Mae's words, "God's got it. He's in control. God is good." As he examined his life, he realized that he must deal with the anger he felt toward his father. Once, in a conversation, his father confided, "You don't know what I've been through, what happened to me." Tyler then remembered that Emmett, his father, had been abandoned in a drainage ditch at the age of two. "When I was able to forgive," says Tyler, "I felt love and compassion for him."

Today, Tyler Perry knows that everything in life, the good and the bad, is a God-given opportunity to stand in the light. "My soul-filled experiences," he says, "have taught me to embrace disappointments, knowing deeper lessons will be revealed. God's hand opens some doors and closes others."

Perry explains that, even now, when he feels he is not hearing God's voice that means something is wrong. "It happened recently," he says. "I was waking up in the morning, watching the news first thing, and being fully captivated by our country's drama and polarization. I allowed myself to become absorbed in it. I got completely caught up in the material world, and put my soul on the back burner. I didn't make time for prayer." He now begins each day with a reverence for God and His blessings, spending the first moments of each day with the One who is Higher.

HILLBILLY ELEGY

I spent the first eighteen years of my life pretending that
everything in the world was a problem except me.
—J. D. Vance, *Hillbilly Elegy*

J. D. Vance was given up for adoption when he was six years old. He writes: "My daddy replaced me with another wife and two children. I never understood how a man could find the *time* to make eight children but can't find the time to support them—virtuous fathers are in short supply."

Following a divorce from Vance's father, his mom married an unemployed high-school dropout, and the couple had violent fights. It was hard for J.D to sleep at night because of the noise, the furniture rocking, heavy stomping, yelling, and sometimes glass-shattering. He began doing poorly in school. "I couldn't tell anyone what was going on, and you never knew when a small childhood transgression would send a plate or book flying across the room. Just one wrong step, and kaboom." Vance describes his life in a world of truly irrational behavior where addictive people destroy what little value exists, where children lose their toys and clothes and self-esteem in support of the addiction. "I was one of those kids with a grim future," he says. "I almost failed out of high school. I nearly gave in to the deep anger and resentment harbored by everyone around me."

During his childhood, Vance's mom rambled in and out of five marriages. The constant moving from house to house, the fighting, and the seemingly endless carousel of new men he and his sister had to meet, learn to love and then forget, was exhausting. When the fighting became too violent and the police were called to handcuff Mom and take her to jail, the children would move in for a while with Mamaw and Papaw. Even though Papaw drank a little too much and Mamaw had her own problems, their home was a true refuge. There was love in that house, a little more peace and quiet, and a routine that would keep the children in school. Mamaw always said to her grandchildren, "You've got to go to college and make something of yourself."

Along with the help of encouraging grandparents, Vance credits a couple of teachers who inspired him to love learning. He says, "A handful of people rescued me." Eventually, someone suggested that joining the Marine Corps could turn him into a disciplined young man; he took that advice and enlisted. "Later he would say, "The Marine Corps taught me how to live like an adult, I learned the importance of physical fitness, personal hygiene, and management of personal finances. But most of all, I learned to try harder and to 'give it all you've got.' There's something powerful about realizing that you've undersold yourself—that somehow your mind confused lack of effort for inability. That's why, when people ask me what I'd most like to change about the white working class, I'd say, 'the feeling that choices don't matter.'"

After years of fearing his own future, of worrying that he would end up like many of his neighbors or family members—addicted to alcohol or drugs, in prison, or with kids he couldn't or wouldn't take care of, his life began to take shape.

In *Hillbilly Elegy,* Vance writes about a culture in crisis—that of many poor white Americans living in abuse, alcoholism, poverty, ignorance, and trauma.

Despite his miserable upbringing, Vance's story is one of success. He is a graduate of Ohio State University and Yale Law School. He has been a contributor to the *National Review* and the *New York Times* and works as an investor at a leading venture capital firm. Here he describes what he considers to be his greatest achievements: "I have a nice job, a happy marriage, a comfortable home, and two lively dogs."

SONYA CARSON

Remember this as you go through life. The person who has the most to do with what happens to you is you! You make the choices; you decide whether you're going to give up or ante up when the going gets tough. Ultimately, it's you who decides whether you will be a success or not, by doing what is legally necessary to get you where you want to go. You are the captain of your own ship. If you don't succeed, you only have yourself to blame.

–Sonya Carson

Ben Carson and his brother Curtis were raised in inner-city Detroit by a mother with a third-grade education. In grade school, the boys lacked motivation and their grades were terrible. Ben had an out-of-control temper that could have landed him in jail. Even though everything around them said otherwise, Sonya Carson was convinced that her sons could make something of their lives.

While living in the slums of Boston, Ben and Curtis became acquainted with roaches, huge rats, and even snakes. On the streets, their very lives were threatened by young white boys simply because they were black. When their mother moved them to Detroit, where they attended a predominately white school, classmates made fun of them because of the clothes they wore. Ben began to think of himself as, "Just a dumb black kid from the poor side of Detroit."

When her boys brought home failing grades, Sonya talked to God about it, and He gave her a plan: Television watching would be restricted to three programs a week, and the boys would spend their time reading library books. Sonya says, "God helped me every step of the way."

By working several jobs at a time, Sonya figured she and her boys would have enough to eat and have a roof over their heads. "While other families would go to movies and amusement parks for entertainment," says Sonya, "we would go to nearby farms and pick strawberries and other fresh produce, offering to pick four bushels for the farmer if he would let us keep one. When we got home, I would can the food so we would have a supply to carry us through the winter."

Ben remembers his mother's constant encouragement: "You weren't born to be a failure, Bennie. You can do it; you just ask the Lord, and He'll help you." When he was eight years old, Ben asked, "Can I be a doctor, mother?" She responded, "If you ask the Lord for something and believe He will do it, then it'll happen."

Dr. Ben Carson is known around the world for breakthroughs in neurosurgery that have brought hope where no hope existed. He was director of pediatric neurosurgery at Johns Hopkins Medical Institution at age thirty-three. His brother Curtis became a successful aeronautical engineer.

UNBROKEN

Forgiveness frees the forgiver. Sometimes we attach our entire lives to the moment we were hurt and allow it to define and consume our very existence. We travel with that hurt, that offense, and brood over it every time it comes to mind. The 'wrong' that has been done to us dictates how

*we speak to our children, our spouses, our friends. Our
hurt continues until we forgive.*

Andy Andrews—*The Heart Mender*

Louis Zamperini, a World War ll veteran, spent two and a half years as a prisoner of war in a Japanese prison camp, experiencing extreme deprivation and torture. His story, written by Laura Hillenbrand, occupied the New York Times Best-Seller List for three years and was made into a major motion picture.

However, the movie ends with the war's end and skips entirely the last chapters of Hillenbrand's book. For many of us who read the book, the post-war stories were most important. In the last chapters, Hillenbrand paints a vivid picture of what happened when Zamperini attended a Billy Graham Crusade, which changed his life completely.

Dr. Billy Graham later became friends with the war hero and recalls conversations with him. "I had the privilege to visit with Louis Zamperini when he was ninety-four years old. He traveled from his home in California to Charlotte, North Carolina, where he graciously appeared at the Billy Graham Library. For several hours he shook people's hands and signed copies of the book *Unbroken,* his life's story. The following day, he rode two hours to my home where we had lunch together. It had been many years since we had visited. Louis patiently answered my questions as I asked him to relay the experiences that led up to his conversion."

Louis told Dr. Graham that when he was a prisoner of war, he doubted that he would ever reach retirement age. Due to brutal treatment in the prison camp, starvation, and psychological trauma, he experienced the challenges of old age prematurely. He told the story of his rescue in 1945, his welcome home as a war hero, and his short-lived celebrity status. He spoke of his frequent nightmares recalling the horrors he experienced as a prisoner. He was drinking heavily, slipping in and out of flashbacks, screaming and clawing through nightmares, and lashing out in fury at random moments. He was obsessed with a desire to return to Japan and destroy Bird, the officer who had tormented him. He said, "I walked around every day with murder in my head."

His wife however, persuaded him to attend the Billy Graham Crusade in Los Angeles, where the Gospel was preached for six straight weeks. He attended the crusade only to please his wife, and slipped out early the first night. On the second night, he planned to leave as soon as the invitation was given. "However," explained Louis, "the Holy Spirit gripped my heart. I walked the aisle into the prayer room where I repented of my sins and gave my life wholly to the Lord Jesus Christ. Within a matter of moments, my life was changed forever. Since that night I have never had another nightmare about my captivity. The Lord radically transformed me."

Later, as Louis prepared to return to Japan to carry the Olympic torch, he also prepared a letter for Bird, the man he had wanted to murder: "Under your discipline, my rights, not only as a prisoner of war but also as a human being, were stripped from me. It was a struggle to maintain enough dignity and hope to live until the war's end. The post-war nightmares caused my life to crumble, but thanks to a confrontation with God through the evangelist Billy Graham, I committed my life to Christ. Love replaced the hate I had for you. Christ said, 'Forgive your enemies and pray for them.' I also forgave you and now hope that you would also become a Christian."

Dr. Graham described the former prisoner of war as, "one of those night-blooming flowers serving the Lord, investing the fruit of his experience in the lives of others." He became an inspirational speaker telling his story to children as well as to many groups of people his own age. His reoccurring theme was always the importance of forgiveness.

Louis Zamperini died July 7, 2014, at the age of 97.

JOSEPH'S DREAMS

Circumstances may appear to wreck our lives and God's plans, but God is not helpless among the ruins, God is still

*working. He comes in and takes the calamity and uses it
victoriously, working out His wonderful plan of love.*
—Eric Liddell, medal-winning Olympic runner
featured in the film "Chariots of Fire"

Joseph spent thirteen years in that horrible place, a dungeon with no
sunlight, just a sunken pit void of light or warmth. The Bible says that
he wore iron shackles that hurt his feet. He was given only bread and
water. There were no showers or bathroom facilities, and prisoners wore
the same stinky clothes day after day. Joseph was thrown into that dungeon to die.

While incarcerated, Joseph had plenty of time to think about his
misfortune—how his brothers had betrayed him and demolished his
dream and that he had not committed a crime and didn't really belong
in jail. He knew he could very well die in that horrible prison.

But Joseph refused to give way to self-pity. Each day, he turned to
God and said, "What would you have me do now, Lord? He knew that
God wanted him to become the very best prisoner he could possibly be
and to look around and see if he could help someone else. Very soon, the
warden put Joseph in charge of all the other prisoners and everything
that happened in prison.

When the time was right, God brought Joseph out of prison and
raised him to a place of honor. He became second in command in the
land of Egypt. Apparently, the prison time was part of the preparation
for the good life God had prepared for him. Eventually, Joseph's brothers
were forced to humble themselves and submit to Joseph's authority.
Although it seemed that Joseph had suffered needlessly because of his
brothers, he was required by God to forgive them. Without forgiveness,
he could not have seen the fulfillment of his God-given dream.

Joseph said to his brothers, "As for you, you thought evil against me,
but God meant it for good to bring about that many people should be
kept alive, as they are this day" (Genesis 50:20).

CHOICES

Your choices, your words, and every move you make are permanent. Life is lived in indelible ink, boy, wake up. You're making little bitty brushstrokes every minute you walk around on this earth. And with those tiny brushstrokes, you are creating the painting. And your life will ultimately become a masterpiece or a disaster.
—Andy Andrews, *The Noticer Returns*

If like Joseph, you have a God-given dream, it will be accomplished according to the daily choices you make. God has given us the gifts and abilities we will need for the journey, but we must walk closely with Him.

In the Book of Genesis, we see Joseph making difficult choices. Somewhere between the pit and Potiphar's house, he chose to be a faithful, obedient slave. When Potiphar's wife made sexual advances, Joseph chose to deny himself and obey God. When he was unjustly thrown into prison, he could have wallowed in self-pity, grumbled, blamed God, and given up on his dream. Yet he chose to focus on meeting the needs of others. When his God-given dream was finally accomplished, his brothers were brought before him, and he had to decide whether to indulge in revenge or to forgive; he chose forgiveness.

Someone has said: "Joseph did not endure the pit, Potiphar's house, and prison because he knew he would end up in Pharoah's palace. He simply remained faithful wherever he found himself. God did the rest."

FEARFUL EYES

I came that they may have and enjoy life, and have it in abundance (to the full, till it overflows).

—Jesus

I watched a scrawny, white cat dart in and out of the woods one winter. I'm sure she was often cold and scared. But when she discovered a dish of milk on my neighbor's porch, kitty ventured closer and became less fearful. In early summer she chose a shady spot at the corner of Miss Opal's yard to give birth to four white kittens. Miss Opal turned a garbage can on its side, put an old quilt inside, and placed an umbrella over the entrance so the felines would have shelter from summer showers. We watched the kittens evolve from squinty-eyed, mouse-like balls of fur, to playful, wide-awake kittens scampering about putting on a lively show while Mother Cat looked on proudly. My grandchildren and I visited their garbage can shelter, petting the kittens and praising the mother— that little family touched our hearts.

After a while, Miss Opal became concerned about the responsibility of caring for the family of five and decided to give some kittens away. A woman came in a yellow car one morning, scooped up two kittens, and drove away. Mother Kitty chased the car for a block. Then she returned to the corner spot and mourned for her lost babies. Watching such grief was too much for Miss Opal to bear; that very same day she reclaimed those kittens and brought them back to their garbage can shelter. Again, Mother Kitty was content.

Then, one day when Miss Opal went down the hill to feed the cats, she suffered a stroke and fell while trying to dish out the food. When she had to go to the hospital, her family decided the kitty family needed new arrangements. One phone call brought the lady with the yellow car. She planned to take Mother Kitty and her babies and let them live together at her house. As she placed the kittens in the box, Mother Kitty watched with anxious eyes. When the lady took a step toward Mother Kitty, she ran. We tried desperately to capture that frantic feline. Later, I caught Kitty and held on tight, but when the lady walked closer, Mother Kitty panicked and dug her claws into my hands so sharply I dropped her and she dashed into the woods. How could we explain our best intentions to a flighty cat? How could she understand that the Lady with the yellow car was offering her a better life?

When I went next door to feed the lonely Mother Kitty, she crouched low in the grass looking up at me with fearful eyes, ready to run if I moved too close. I told her I was sorry she lost her babies, but she didn't understand what I was saying.

I've seen people wander through this world just like that cat. They've been cold and scared and kicked around; fear fills their eyes as they struggle to fend for themselves. I've seen God reach down to touch their lives, but they turned away and ran back to their old garbage can shelters. Maybe they didn't understand what God was saying.

Chapter Three

Amazing Mind

Life consists of what a man is thinking all day.
—Ralph Waldo Emerson

You are today where your thoughts have brought you. You will be tomorrow where your thoughts take you.
—James Allen

Whatever thoughts are true, noble, just, pure, lovely, are of good report, if there is any virtue and if there is anything praiseworthy; think on these things.
—Paul The Apostle

Nurture great thoughts, for you will never go higher than your thoughts.
—Benjamin Disraeli

Everything begins with a thought. What we think determines who we are, who we are determines what we do, and our thoughts determine our destiny. We can change the way we think.
—John Maxwell, *Thinking for a Change*

YOU HAVE A BRAIN

The size of a grapefruit, at the top of our spinal column, it weighs about three pounds. Nobody tells us it is the most complex piece of matter yet found in the universe. Nobody tells us that it is a miracle and that we are miracles.

The possibility that this amazing human brain would evolve randomly from the chemical ooze of primeval oceans to what it is today, the probability of this happening merely by chance is about the same as the probability of a tornado blowing through a junkyard and randomly assembling a fully functioning Boeing 747 jumbo jet.

Nobody suggests that the human brain is a miracle, and that we are miracles. Nobody tells us that we might dream greater dreams than the little plastic and tinsel we have been offered. Nobody acts amazed. Mostly, we just blunder on –bored miracles.

—G. Lynn Nelson, *Writing and Being*

Dr. Benjamin Carson, former director of neurosurgery at Johns Hopkins Hospital, says, "Every time I've opened a child's head and seen the brain, I marvel at the mystery. This is what makes every one of us who we are. This is what holds all our memories, all our thoughts, and all our dreams. This is what makes us different from each other in many ways."

In his book *You Have a Brain,* Carson writes, "God has given to every one of us more than fourteen billion cells and connections in our brain. This most complex organ system in the entire universe is a tremendous gift from God." He explains that the brain sorts, organizes, and warehouses that deluge of sensory data flooding in at millions of bytes per second. It's the control and command center for all our senses, all our other organs, our body temperature, and the operation of every system in the human body. Most of this work the brain does automatically without a thought from us. On top of all that, the brain enables us to imagine, create, and solve problems. "We're the only creatures on earth with the capacity to analyze, strategize, and prioritize," says Carson, "so, we can alter or improve the world around us."

God has given us everything we need to think big. "He is what ties it all together," writes Carson. "So, the better we know the One who designed our brains, the bigger and better we'll be able to think. Because we cannot ever think bigger than God."

In his book, *Think Big,* Carson writes of the influence his mother had on the way he learned to think. Sonya Carson would say, "Ben, you are a smart boy. I want to see you using that smartness. You can become whatever you want to be in this life if you're willing to work at it. I work among rich people who are educated. I watch how they act and I know you can do anything they can do, only you must try to do it better." She demanded that Ben and Curtis replace television watching with the reading of books. They were required to read two books from the library each week and to write about what they had read. This became a lifelong habit. Dr. Carson says, "In my opinion, the base of personal preparation comes more from reading than from any other source. We cannot read too much and most of us do not read enough." He recommends daily Bible reading, saying, "For me, the most important and regular source of insight comes from the book of Proverbs. I suggest reading and rereading Proverbs, together with the entire Bible."

THE MOST VALUABLE TROPHY

You formed my innermost being, shaping my delicate inside and my intricate outside, and wove them all together in my mother's womb. Everything You do is marvelously breathtaking.

—Psalm 139:13-14 Passion Bible

The subject of brain health is examined in the book *Age Smart,* written by Dr. Jeffrey Rosensweig and Betty Liu. They tell us to protect our brain as if it's the most valuable trophy in the world. When these authors interviewed Dr. Johnetta Cole, former president of Bennett College, she said, "To many of us, our mind represents the essence of our being." She admits that her biggest fear would be to lose the capacity to be engaged mentally. "Obviously, I don't look forward to physical infirmities," said Cole, "but the ability to read, to write, and to think are really very central to my sense of myself and to my happiness."

Rosensweig and Liu tell us that those who stay mentally challenged throughout their lives have a much better chance to remain mentally sharp until the very end of their lives. Your brain is just like every other muscle in your body; if you don't use it, it will get weak. It will become more susceptible to wear and tear; the longer you stop exercising it, the harder it'll be to get it back into good shape. If your brain is not kept running and stimulated, the dendrites—those tree-like extensions of a neuron that receive information from other neurons, actually atrophy. You literally lose mass.

Age Smart also suggests that it is just as much of a chore to exercise your brain as it is to exercise your body. Researchers equate television watching with an absence of cognitive processing. When you watch television, you do nothing for the brain. Researchers have found that when people use their brains in unusual ways, blood flows into different neural regions and creates new connections. For example, if you are a writer, you can exercise the right part of the brain by learning how to fix a car.

YOU CAN BUILD A BETTER BRAIN!

What's good for the heart is good for the brain.
                                        –Dr. Sanjay Gupta

In the book *Keep Sharp: Build a Better Brain at Any Age, Dr. Sanjay Gupta* instructs us to eat well, exercise often, get proper rest, and live with a sense of purpose. These things are not only good for our physical well-being but can help to build and restore the brain.

Regarding food, Dr. Gupta says, "What's good for the heart is good for the brain." Eat fresh vegetables, in particular, leafy greens such as spinach, chard, kale, arugula, collard greens, mustard greens, romaine lettuce, Swiss chard, turnip greens, as well as whole berries, fish and sea-food, and healthy fats such as extra virgin olive oil, avocadoes, whole eggs, nuts, and seeds. Also, include beans and other legumes, whole fruits, low-fat dairy products such as yogurt and cottage cheese, poultry, and whole grains. We should limit fried food, pastries, sugary foods, processed foods, red meat, whole-fat high in saturated fat, such as cheese and butter, and salt.

Dr. Gupta explains that exercise is just as important for the brain as for the body. "When people ask me what's the single most important thing they can do to enhance their brain's function and resiliency to dis-ease," says Dr. Gupta, "I answer with one word: Exercise—as in move more and keep a regular physical fitness routine. Fitness could very well be the most important ingredient to living as long as possible." He tells us that physical exercise is the only behavioral activity scientifically proven to trigger biological effects that can help the brain, and that we would all do well to get in motion. It is never too late to start. Swimming, cycling, jogging, walking, dancing, hiking or gardening. Brisk walking at least five days a week for at least twenty minutes is a good way to start.

Dr. Gupta says, "A well-rested brain is a healthy brain." He explains that sleep is anything but a waste of time. It's when the body heals tissues, strengthens memory, and even grows. Losing sleep will have both short and long-term consequences on your health. He warns, "You cannot necessarily catch up on sleep later on by sleeping in over the weekend or taking a long, sleepy vacation."

Dr. Gupta believes that living with a sense of purpose is very important—your reason for being. After all, isn't that what gets us out of bed every morning? He says, "With purpose comes the motivation to remain physically active and to take better care of yourself. Purpose puts a damper on depression, which can be common in one's later years."

DO YOU RECOGNIZE THE VOICE?

*My own sheep will hear my voice and I know each one,
and they will follow me.*
—John 10:27

Thoughts, words, and impressions come silently into my mind each day. There are two voices. One is God's voice; the other is the voice of my enemy Satan. The latter comes to "Steal, Kill, and Destroy." But God's voice comes to give me Abundant Life. I must continually make choices about which voices I will listen to and believe. The thoughts I choose to believe will determine my future.

In her book, *Finding Water,* Julia Cameron reveals her thoughts:

"The Devil always comes to me through despair. The Devil talks about the odds stacked against me and how foolish I have been. The Devil likes to say: 'What's the use? Game over.' The Devil comes to me, above all, as a drink. The Devil wants me to think that if I just had a drink, everything will be better, at least more bearable. There is nothing that taking a drink is going to make better. The Devil tells me I am about to lose everything and I think that perhaps I am. The Devil would certainly like to paralyze me with fear so that losing things becomes more likely."

In the book *God Calling,* there is a great example of God's voice:

"Come to Me with a teachable spirit, eager to be changed. A close walk with Me is a life of continual newness. Do not cling to the old ways. Seek My face with an open mind, knowing that your journey with Me involves being transformed by the renewing of your mind. I know you and understand you completely. I know the plans I have for you; plans to prosper you and not to harm you, plans to give you hope and a future."

God's voice comes from the pages of the Bible. If we meditate on the scriptures long enough, the enemy voice will begin to fade away.

MIND CHATTER

Literally, everything that goes into your mind has an effect. It either builds or prepares you for the future or it tears down and reduces your accomplishments.

—Zig Ziglar

Do you ever talk to yourself? Does everyone talk to themselves? Do tough times make our negative chatter worse? Elizabeth Bernstein, a writer for the Wall Street Journal Newspaper, asked these questions of experimental psychologist Ethan Kross, who has written a book about self-talk called "Chatter: The voice in your head."

Kross explains that we all talk silently to ourselves every day: "We do it to keep things fresh in our heads, like repeating a phone number, or we try to simulate what we are planning to say, like when we go on an interview." However, he says, our self-talk can sabotage us, when we 'chatter' in our head trying to find the answer to a problem, but end up making the problem worse.

Kross admits that tough times can make our negative chatter worse, saying "The year 2020 was the chatter event of the century. Political instability. A once-in-a-hundred-years virus that caused us to refrain from socializing directly with others. We experienced political divisiveness, unemployment, and a shaky economy."

When asked how we can control the negative chatter in our minds, Kross says there is a lot of research that shows we are much better at advising other people than ourselves. He suggests, "It can help to think of yourself as if you are someone else. Use distanced self-talk and coach yourself as if you were advising a friend."

Christian speaker Joyce Meyer writes about the "Battlefield of the Mind." She says, "Sometimes we have to reason with ourselves. When strange feelings threaten to overwhelm us, we need to stop and take control of our thoughts and feelings. One way we do that is by talking to ourselves." She speaks of a time when she dealt with feelings of loneliness. She began to say to herself, "Joyce, knock it off! You may feel lonely, but you are not alone. Think of all the people God has put in your life." She then begins thanking God for each friend.

My friend tells me that when worries continue recycling through her mind, she sits down and writes a letter to God. She writes about her doubts and fears, and then, she listens for God's voice as she reads her Bible.

We are responsible for the chatter in our minds. We are able to delete worry thoughts and replace them with God-thoughts.

BEDTIME STORIES

I have sweet memories of cuddling in the covers with my grandchildren on winter nights, pajamas and bare feet, little cheeks smelling like soap fresh from the bathtub, a stack of books waiting to be read before lights out. One of our favorite bedtime stories, written by Irene Keller, went something like this:

Benjamin Rabbit had a hard time sleeping at night because he was convinced there was a monster under his bed. Benjamin could see it. It was large as life, and as big as a house, with one huge red-eye right in the middle of its forehead. And it was looking right at Benjamin!

When Benjamin cried out to Mother Rabbit, she came quickly and brought a "Monster Remover." Even though it looked and smelled much like a can of air freshener, when Mother turned on the light and sprayed great swooshes of Monster Remover under the bed, the intruder disappeared. When the room was flooded with light, Mother Rabbit said, "See, it wasn't a monster. It was only the moon shining on your bicycle reflector. It just looked like a big red eye!"

Recently, while having a restless night, I remembered Benjamin's dilemma. At three o'clock in the morning, there was something like a monster in my bedroom. Unlike Benjamin's monster, my unwelcome intruder did not hide under the bed, but rather boldly perched upon my shoulder and began filling my mind with foreboding thoughts. He told me that my future would be much worse than my past and that it was my fault because I was inadequate in every way. His most impressive lie was that my current problem was unsolvable and that God no longer heard my prayers.

Although I am, by day, a sensible grownup grandmother, the truth is those condemning thoughts are just as real to me on a dark night as Benjamin Rabbit's red-eyed monster was to him. I meditated on those words, and the more I thought about it, they made perfect sense! My problems did seem impossible, there were apparently no answers, and I asked myself the question, "If God is listening, why hasn't He answered my prayers already?"

I became more and more agitated and fear dominated my mind. I tossed and turned, but I could not shake that silly voice off my shoulder. There was nothing to do but get out of bed and turn on a light. With the click of the light, my monster thoughts began to retreat. And when

I opened my Bible and began praying, I then saw my silly monster as clearly as Mother Rabbit had seen that harmless bicycle reflector.

I read: "For I know the plans I have for you," says the Lord. "They are plans for good and not for disaster, to give you a future and a hope. When you pray, I will listen. If you look for Me wholeheartedly, you will find me" (Jeremiah 29:11-13).

> "He who dwells in the secret place of the Most High shall abide under the shadow of the Almighty. I will say of the Lord, "He is my refuge and my fortress; My God, in Him I will trust."

> "You shall not be afraid of the terror by night, nor of the arrow that flies by day, nor of the pestilence (deadly epidemic disease) that walks in darkness, nor of the destruction that lays waste at noonday... No evil shall befall you, nor shall any plague come near your dwelling... He shall call upon Me, and I will answer him; I will be with him in trouble. With long life will I satisfy him, and show him My salvation" (Psalm 91).

WINTERY FEELINGS

You can't always believe everything you think.
— Andy Andrews, *Just Jones*

It's the dead of winter. The trees are empty, it's been cold and rainy, the days are short with less daylight, and spring seems so far away. When the sun is shrouded with dark clouds and nights are long and cold, feelings of depression can be so near.

Dreary winter days are good for reading books by the fire, so recently I reread some of Andy Andrews' books. They give hope with a Christian lifestyle view. He writes fiction, inserting words of wisdom, often drawing from the lives of historical figures. In one of his books, I learned that some very famous people suffered from depression. According to Andrews, Winston Churchill's depression often brought thoughts of suicide. He said this state of mind was like a "black dog" that followed him.

Churchill describes his negative feelings as visiting "the valley of the shadow of death" where he was allowed to think and brood over his problems. In Andrews' book, "The Final Summit," Churchill says, "The black dog wasn't always with me, wasn't always in sight, but I grew to find that he was ever nearby. I learned to be on my guard. I never liked standing near the edge of a platform when an express train was passing through. I always stood far back and, if possible, got a pillar between the train and me. I wouldn't allow myself to stand by the side of a ship and look down into the water. A second's action could have ended everything."

However, Churchill would not permit his feelings to destroy his life. He offered this wisdom: "We experience loneliness and gain humility, but then we learn to focus our thoughts on others and not weep for ourselves." He also said, "I have long believed that there are no hopeless situations; there are only people who have grown hopeless about them."

Also, in *The Final Summit,* Abraham Lincoln admits that for him depression was a common state of mind until he learned that he could discipline himself to feel differently. It seems Lincoln believed that cheerfulness is a result of self-discipline. "We have a choice, we can sleep, avoid people, brood, and think about how depressed we are. In so doing, we are feeding the thing that can destroy life." Lincoln learned to walk instead of sleep. He learned to enjoy the company of certain people instead of brooding alone, and to read good books and listen to happy music instead of reflecting sorrowfully on his feelings of depression. He said, "Of course, you don't feel like doing these things, but can you make yourself do what you don't feel like doing? This is discipline."

Another character in Andrew's book is King David. From the Book of Psalms, we see that when David felt gloomy and hopeless, he cried out to God: "My God, My God, why have You forsaken me? Why are You so far from helping me, and from the words of my groaning?" Later, his faith is restored, and he says, "I waited patiently for the Lord, and He inclined to me, and heard my cry. He also brought me up out of a horrible pit and set my feet upon a rock, and established my steps." Psalm 40:1-2

The dead of winter is only a season, and spring always follows. We will cry out to God and wait, "For lo, the winter is past, the rain is over and gone. The flowers appear on the earth; the time of singing has come." Song of Solomon 2:11-12

START WHERE YOU ARE

When I open my calendar to a new year, nothing magical happens, my problems have not disappeared. But because it's a new year, it's like I have another chance to begin again. I'm actually writing the story of my life, not for a book for someone to read, but hour by hour, day by day, I'm living my story. Every day of my life is important to God because He brought me into this world with a purpose and a plan. He arranged for me to be where I am in this very hour, on the street where I live, in the church I attend, and in the company of friends and acquaintances. And all the while, I am writing on the slate that God gave me. I'm telling my story, choice by choice, step by step.

On Christmas day, our family watched "It's a Wonderful Life." Although we've seen it many times, the message is always new again. The main character, George Bailey, (Jimmy Stewart) is threatened with bankruptcy and time in jail. He despairs of what he has made of his life and attempts suicide on Christmas Eve. However, George has been assigned an angel who intervenes. Clarence, the angel, prevents disaster and allows George to see how much worse the world would have been if he was never born.

As I watched the happy ending of the movie, I began examining my own life and the effect it might have had on others. I remembered many things I should have done differently. I made a lot of mistakes. I missed opportunities to do good, spoke words I should not have spoken, wasted valuable time, and the list goes on. However, I can make a choice to learn from past mistakes and begin again.

Rashawn Copeland, in his book, *Start Where You Are,* says, "God meets you in your mess, loves you through it, and leads you out of it. You were made to be blessed by God and sent to bless others." This insight came to Copeland after a close call with suicide. He tells his story: "I walk down the hall, get the gun, and walk back to my bedroom. No one else is home. No one will stop me. I put the gun barrel in my mouth. I take it out again. I reach for my phone, and Facebook is the only app I see. I absentmindedly click on it, and there it is—the post that saves my life."

He explains: "I only followed one Christian on Facebook. I'd met her once at a party. Now, she was speaking powerfully through a Facebook post in my darkest hour. The scripture she had posted spoke to my heart. I read it again and again and again. I forgot all about the gun. I fell onto my face before God."

Copeland says, "Within days of my conversion I returned home with nothing but a heart full of new possibilities. I didn't know where I was going but I knew where to start: right where I was."

When we fall on our faces before God in total surrender, He meets us in the middle of the mess we've made. He is there to love us through all the troubles, to lead us out, and to help us write better stories in each new year.

THE POWER OF WORDS

Words, so innocent and powerless as they are, standing in a dictionary, how potent for good and evil they become in the hands of one who knows how to combine them.
                                    –Nathaniel Hawthorne

The two most important days in your life are the day you were born and the day you find out why.
                                    –Mark Twain

He had always believed himself to be an inadequate person. He was so shy when company came to visit his family, he would run and hide in the woodshed. College was really difficult for him. When required to give a presentation in front of the class, he would make a miserable showing. His professor followed him out of class one day and said some tough but true things. The young man will never forget those words. "The professor said that I had a reasonably good mind, but that I was not making adequate use of it by being so hesitant and bashful. He demanded, 'How long are you going to be like this, a scared rabbit, afraid of your own voice? You probably just excuse yourself by thinking that you are just naturally shy. Well, you'd better change the way you think about yourself, and you'd better do it now before it's too late. If you need help, well, you're a minister's son."

Following this, the young man felt angry and resentful and said, "I was hurt, but most of all I was frightened because I knew that what the professor had said was true. A scared rabbit! How far would I get in life if I kept seeing myself as a scared rabbit?"

The young man then sat down on the steps of the chapel and prayed the deepest, most desperate prayer of his whole life. "Please help me," he said, "Please change me. I know you can do it because I've seen you make drunkards sober and turn thieves into honest men. Please take away these inferiority feelings. Give me the strength and the confidence I need."

Later, the young man would write: "The dynamic laws which my book teaches were learned the hard way, by trial and error, in my personal search for a way of life. But I found them in answer to my own problems and, believe me, I am the most difficult person with whom I have ever worked. I found my own answers in the teachings of Jesus Christ."

The little boy grew up and became Dr. Norman Vincent Peale. He found the solution to his problems in the simple techniques taught in the Bible. He said, "These principles are scientific and sound and can heal any personality of the pain of inferiority feelings."

In his book, *The Power of Positive Thinking,* Dr. Peale emphasized the importance of faith in the God of the Bible. He wrote, "You can overcome any obstacle. You can achieve the most tremendous things by faith power. You must saturate your mind with the great words of the Bible." His instructions were to spend one hour a day by reading the Bible and committing its great passages to memory, thus allowing them to recondition your personality. He also instructed: "Pray deep, big prayers that have plenty of suction, and you will come up with powerful and vital faith." His famous book instructs us to replace thoughts of insecurity and inadequacy with thoughts from God's Word.

Peale said that his first book was written for the plain people of this world. Having been born in humble midwestern circumstances in a dedicated Christian home, he considered himself one of those plain people. *The Power of Positive Thinking* was first published in 1952. It became widely read, and although it received frequent criticism from some church leaders, it continues to be read by millions across the world today.

LIFE CHANGING WORDS

Words are the most powerful tools at our disposal. With them, writers have saved lives and taken them, brought justice and confounded it, raised armies, started wars and ended them. writers can change minds, alter the way people think, and transform our definition of right and wrong.

—Mary Pipher

What words are we hearing? What are we reading? What are we speaking to our children? Those little people don't know who they are yet, but they are learning from the words and actions of the people around them. Words plant ideas in their subconscious, for good or for bad, for hurt or for healing.

Our children pass on the words that surround them. A first-grade teacher tells me that she can tell from listening to her students what their home life is like. She can see which families value kindness and manners. She can determine if her students are loved and secure at home. She can even tell if a child is read to at home, or if the parents act out in fear in scary situations like thunderstorms. She knows how those children are spoken to by the way they speak to others.

As children become adults, words follow them and often shape their futures. My friend Curtis told me that when he was a child, his father always said, "You ain't never gonna amount to nothing!" Those words were not true, but the little boy did not know that. After all, his father had said it and surely a boy's father ought to know. So, for years, Curtis lived according to his father's prediction. He saw himself as a person not able to accomplish anything worthwhile and he felt that everyone else saw him that way also. He did badly in school and dropped out before graduating. He became a heavy drinker, got into fights, went to jail, and eventually lived in a homeless shelter.

However, it was at the homeless shelter where he heard words that changed his life. Curtis told me that there was a suicidal man in the shelter, and a minister had been called to counsel with him. Curtis overheard the minister say to the suicidal man, "Please don't end your life. No matter where you've been, God loves you and He has a plan for your life." Curtis took that advice for himself that very night. He followed that pastor to church, began to follow Jesus, and became a very special man.

Many years ago, there was a little boy who lived with his mother in the mountains of Tennessee. His mom was not married, and in those days, being an illegitimate child afforded the town gossips a chance to harass mother and child. With sly grins, they would ask, "Hey boy, who is your daddy?"

The kids at school heard the gossip from their parents, and continually bullied the little boy with hurtful words. So, the boy would try to hide from the school kids, he would avoid going out in public, and on Sundays, he would sit on the back row in church and slip out early to avoid the question, "Hey, boy, who's your daddy?" Oh, how he dreaded that question.

When the boy was twelve years old, a new pastor came to the church. On the first day with the new pastor, when the service was over, the boy was trapped in the crowd and forced to walk by the pastor on his way out.

The new pastor asked the dreaded question: "Hi son, who is your daddy?" After an awkward moment of silence, the pastor then said, "Oh I know who you are. I see the family resemblance now. You are a child of God!" He then took the boy by the shoulders and said, "Son you have a great inheritance. Go and claim it."

Ben Hooper said those words changed his life. He grew up and became the Governor of Tennessee.

In *The Right Words at the Right Time,* Marlow Thomas wrote, "The perfect turn of a phrase, spoken at precisely the right moment, makes a difference in a life. Words can change a life in an eyeblink." Her book offers a series of stories where people contribute their success in life to words spoken to them. My favorite story in Marlow Thomas' book is Carly Simon's.

When she was a child, Carly had a terrible stuttering problem. "By the time I reached the fourth grade," says Carly, "the problem had reached a critical level. It was awful. I dreaded being made fun of by my classmates. I'd hide in my bedroom, under the bed, anything I could do not to have to go to school." She remembers sitting at the dinner table unable to speak the words, "Pass the butter." She tried again and again, but could not get the words out. So, her mother said, "Sing it, Carly." She did just that, completing the sentence in one try. "My mother gave me the most valuable advice of all that year," says Carly. "She sat me down and said, "If you can start thinking of other people rather than yourself all the time, you may begin to lose your self-consciousness."

Carly Simon became one of the most gifted singer-songwriters of her time.

HARRIET BEECHER STOWE

You write in order to change the world, knowing perfectly well that you probably can't, but also knowing that literature is indispensable to the world... The world changes according to the way people see it, and if you alter, even by a millimeter, the way... people look at reality, then you can change it.

–James Baldwin

Many believe that Harriet Beecher Stowe literally changed the course of American history with her book *Uncle Tom's Cabin*. In a biography, Noel B. Gerson says, "Her pen produced a document that, though far less concise than the Declaration of Independence, was almost equally influential in shaping the destiny of her country and the world."

Raised in the Beecher family, Harriet was encouraged to read widely and to become devoted to the betterment of mankind and social justice.

She once saw a slave family torn apart, the father sold to one buyer, the mother to another, and then a three-year-old child left without parents. Gerson tells us, "Unable to tolerate the injustice, Harriet Beecher Stowe borrowed the money to buy the child and was able to reunite her with her mother."

On a Sunday morning in February 1851, as Harriet attended a communion service at the College Chapel, a vision suddenly filled her mind. She saw an old slave being subjected to a brutal beating, while his tormentor was urged to further excesses by another white man. And then the scene changed, and she saw the dying slave forgive his murderers as he prayed for the salvation of their souls.

Harriet said, "I could not control the story; it wrote itself. The Lord himself wrote it, and I was the humblest of instruments in His Hand. To Him alone should be given the praise."

Russian writer Leo Tolstoy would later compare her story with that of *A Tale of Two Cities and Les Misérables.* Queen Victoria read it and became an ardent admirer. Elizabeth Barrett Browning said to Harriet, "You have done so much to set this accursed slavery in the glare of the world. They should raise a statue to you in America and elsewhere."

As hearts were changed by the words of her novel, Harriet Beecher Stowe would become one of the greatest celebrities of the nineteenth century.

Chapter Four

So Many Books

———✧✦✧———

*When you read, your mind must work by taking in let-
ters and connecting them to form words. Words make
themselves into thoughts and concepts. Developing good
reading habits is something like being a champion weight-
lifter. The champion didn't go into the gym one day and
start lifting 500 pounds. He toned his muscles, beginning
with lighter weights, always building up, preparing for
more. It's the same thing for intellectual feats. We develop
our minds by reading, by thinking, by figuring out things
for ourselves.*

—Ben Carson, M.D., Gifted Hands

THE BIBLE

*The book to read is not the one which thinks for you, but
the one which makes you think. No book in the world
equals the Bible for that.*

—James McCosh

"The Bible is the most powerful book in the world. It is remarkable in its composition. Composed over sixteen centuries by forty authors, written by soldiers, shepherds, farmers, and fishermen. Begun by Moses in Arabia and finished by John on Patmos. Penned by kings in palaces, shepherds in tents, and prisoners in prisons. Would it be possible for forty writers, largely unknown to each other, writing in three different languages and several different countries, separated in time by as much as sixteen-hundred years, to produce a book of singular theme unless behind them there was one mind and one designer?

> "It is remarkable in durability. It is the single most published book in history, translated into at least twelve hundred languages by an army of translators. It has outlived all its opponents. Bibles have been burned by governments and banished from courtrooms, but God's Word endures. The death knell has been sounded a hundred times, but God's Word continues. It is remarkable in prophecy. Its pages contain more than three hundred fulfilled prophecies about the life of Christ, yet they were all written before He was born."
>
> –Max Lucado, *Glory Days*

The Bible is our textbook, our directions for living this life God has given us. The Bible contains a life-giving message each day for each believer. When we combine prayer with the reading of the Word, God gives directions for our journey through life. He directs our steps as we listen and obey. This is the most important book to read, and it should be read daily.

READING FOR LIFE

I cannot remember a time when I was not in love with them—with the books themselves, cover and binding and the paper they were printed on, with their smell and their weight and with their possession in my arms, captured and carried off to myself.

–Eudora Welty

In first grade, I was introduced to *Dick* and *Jane*. Those little red, green and yellow pages made me happy; I was learning to read. However, my fascination with books and stories actually began in fifth grade, when my teacher, Mrs. Flossie Shackelford, read to me from *Little Women*. That very first day in her classroom while listening to her voice, I fell in love with books. *Little Women* led me on a pathway to a wonderful place—the public library. Years later, in the pages of *A Tree Grows in Brooklyn,* I found someone like me—Francie Nolan. The library was Francie's favorite place: She said, *"The feeling I had about it was as good as the feeling I had about church."* Francie thought that all the books in the world were in that library and she had a plan for reading every one of them. She would read a book a day in alphabetical order, and "not skip the dry ones," reading from A to Z. Francie had heard her daddy say that no one in his family had ever gone to college. Francie wanted to do better. Her mother said that all the knowledge in the world could be found in books, and mother had a plan—every night before they went to bed, Francie and her brother were to read a page of the Bible and a page of Shakespeare.

I've read *a Tree Grows in Brooklyn* more than once. And once, I stayed up all night reading *Gone with the Wind*. From my book shelf, I retrieve Bronte's *Jane Eyre* to read a third time, as well as *Galway Bay*, by Mary Pat Kelly. Fiction began teaching me about life and that I was not alone with my thoughts and feelings. But eventually, in my library wanderings, I also found priceless wisdom in nonfiction. *The Power of*

Positive Thinking, by Norman Vincent Peale, changed my life. I was surprised to find that it was filled with scripture. In reading it, I gained a new awareness of the bold fact that the Bible is actually God speaking to me, telling me things I need to know and how to live my life. Peale's *The Power of Positive Thinking* led me straight to the Bible.

Now, as I search through my bookshelves, I find books that have been stepping stones, taking me to new places, introducing me to people who would add value to my life, and opening my eyes to things I had been too blind to see.

If I had never read Harriet Beecher Stowe's *Uncle Tom's Cabin* or *Black Boy* by Richard Wright, I would not be able to see into the hearts of my brothers and sisters of color. I have enjoyed Charles Dickens' stories because of his priceless wit which makes me laugh out loud sometimes, but he has also taken me into the streets of London, where I have seen the chimney-sweep kids, and wept for them.

The books that have encouraged my prayer life are priceless. I read the life of George Mueller, the founder of orphanages in England. This amazing biography is about a man who recorded his prayer requests in journals and received answers to all his prayers. *My Glimpse of Eternity,* by Betty Malz, gave me a vivid picture of prayer. Dutch Sheets explains the process of prayer in *Intercessory Prayer* and tells of miracles that happen when people pray persistently. Mark Batterson's book, *The Circle Maker* is a true inspiration. In Frank Peretti's novel, *This Present Darkness,* I saw that God's angels stand waiting to help us in times of trouble, but often, they can do nothing until we pray to God the Father, in the name of Jesus.

In biographies, the lives of great people have inspired me. Charismatic Christians like John G. Lake and Smith Wigglesworth participated in amazing miracles. I believe the stories of George Washington Carver's life should be required reading for high school students, along with *Gifted Hands* by Dr. Benjamin Carson. Among favorite memoirs are those of Pulitzer Prize-winning author Frank McCourt, who wrote *Angela's Ashes, Tis, and Teacher Man.* Rick Bragg's writings are priceless;

I have read *All Over but the Shouting, Ava's Man, and Somebody Told Me,* all three, more than once. For pure enjoyment, I return to *My Cat, Spit Magee,* by Willie Morris.

My favorite books on creativity are *Lightposts for Living* by Thomas Kinkade and a collection of books by Julia Cameron. I read and reread books on the craft of writing by Julia Cameron, Brenda Euland, and Madeline L'Engle.

My favorite fiction writers are Jan Karon, Francine Rivers, Andy Andrews, and Irish writers, Rosamunde Pilcher, and Maeve Binchy.

Short stories by Eudora Welty and William Faulkner are more appealing to me than their novels. I could never forget Welty's *The Worn Path* or Faulkner's *A Rose for Emily.*

For a renewing of my mind, I read the Bible daily.

THE EDUCATION OF A WANDERING MAN

We are often told that we are what we eat. In our world since the printing press, it might be more accurate to say we are what we read.
    –Louis L'Amour, *The Education of a Wandering Man*

Today there are more than 300 million copies of Louis L'Amour's books in print worldwide. They have been translated into 20 languages, and many have been made into movies. This is an amazing accomplishment for a man who, because of financial needs, left school when he was only halfway through the tenth grade and never attended college. Yet, through constant reading and traveling he acquired a remarkable education.

L'Amour's education began in his childhood home, where reading seemed to be as natural as breathing. "Ours was a family in which everybody was constantly reading, and where literature, politics, and the events of the prize ring were discussed at breakfast, lunch, and dinner," said L'Amour. "How many books we had in our home I do not remember.

65

We had collections of Longfellow, Whittier, Lowell and Emerson. All of us had library cards, and they were always in use."

L'Amour's father gave him a three-volume *History of the World*. These books had come as a premium with a subscription to *Colliers Magazine*. He recalls, "For the next three months when my father came home, I would sit on his knee and tell him what I had read that day."

In his autobiography, L'Amour tells of hoboing across the country on the Southern Pacific Railway during the Great Depression. He explains that a hobo was not a bum or a tramp, but rather a wandering worker, and therefore, a person who was essential to the nation's economy at that time. Often, men riding on freight trains would share stories, trade books, and spend much of their time reading.

L'Amour says, "Education is available to anyone within reach of a library, a post office, or even a newsstand. You can buy a fair beginning of an education in any bookstore with a good stock of paperback books. Often, I hear people say they don't have time to read. That's absolute nonsense." He adds, "Books are precious things, but more than that, they are the backbone of civilization." Throughout his life, the Wandering Man read the Bible several times.

Chapter Five

It's Never Too Late

❧

Retirement is a time to tackle projects and unlock dreams, a time to revisit the past and explore the unknown. It is time to design our future. Laura Ingalls Wilder published Little House in the Big Woods *when she was sixty-four. B.B. King toured until six months before his death at age eighty-nine. At age eighty-nine, Arthur Rubenstein had given one of his most enthralling recitals, in Carnegie Hall. At eighty-two, Churchill wrote* A History of the English-Speaking People, *in four volumes. Grandma Moses was still painting and getting paid for it at the age of one-hundred.*

–Julia Cameron, It's Never Too Late to Begin Again

GRANDMA MOSES

The world is waiting for that special contribution each of us was born to make.

–Marlyn Kondwoni

67

The above quote is typical of those made at Graduation ceremonies. Perhaps we believe it is meant only for young people who are just beginning their lives. Not so! It could very well apply to those of us who have reached Senior Citizen status. Claude Pepper, a member of the U.S. House of Representatives in 1962, said "Life is like riding a bicycle. You don't fall off until you stop pedaling." Quite often we're pedaling along just fine, then, wham! Suddenly, life knocks us down. We feel pain, fear, and disappointment—we feel old. Nevertheless, with a prayer, some struggle, and a little time, we can climb back up and try again. I am always encouraged when I read about people who actually did that and lived successfully to a ripe old age, all the while, contributing something of value to their corner of the world. The story of Grandma Moses inspires me:

Ann Mary Moses gave birth to ten children; five of them died. She and her husband worked as tenant farmers while raising their family. In her hunger for beauty, she began embroidering. After her husband died, her fingers became stiff with arthritis, and she could no longer accomplish the stitches. Searching for a way to use her creativity, she found herself painting colorful pictures on barn wood. After the age of seventy, she produced more than sixteen hundred paintings. When she was one hundred years old, she painted book illustrations for *Twas the Night Before Christmas*.

When Grandma Moses was interviewed by Edward R. Murrow on his radio program, "See It Now," she said, "If I didn't start painting, I would have raised chickens. I would never sit back in a rocking chair waiting for someone to help me." This amazing woman lived to be 101. Her work is still in circulation today. She concluded her autobiography, *My Life History,* with the following words:

"I look back on my life like a good day's work, it was done and I feel satisfied with it. I was happy and contented; I knew nothing better and made the best out of what life offered. And life is what we make it, always has been, always will be."

Although we do not all have the artistic gifts of Grandma Moses, perhaps there's something special each of us is destined to add to our corner of the world in the later years of our lives. I know grandmothers who are raising grandchildren to become godly citizens who contribute to society and the Christian community. I know mothers and grand-mothers whose prayers are availing much.

Best-selling author Mark Batterson writes about his grandfather who would take off his hearing aids each night, kneel by his bed, and pray very loudly for his grandchildren. Mark says, "My grandfather died when I was six, but his prayers did not. There have been distinct moments in my life when I've received a blessing I didn't deserve, and the Holy Spirit has whispered these words: 'Mark, the prayers of your grandfather are being answered in your life right now.'"

AGELESS SPIRIT

Find a reason to get up every morning, something that takes your mind off yourself, then get up every day and do it.
–Alice L. Moseley

After watching the morning sun make sparkles on the water, we turned off the beach road and drove along a quiet street in Bay St. Louis searching for a blue house where a famous folk artist lived. Our hostess at the Bed and Breakfast where we were staying had called ahead to announce our visit. Ninety-four-year-old Mrs. Alice Moseley, petite and perky, dressed in blue pants, a red vest, and sporting a red beret in her pretty white hair, waited for us on her front porch. We walked past a white picket fence lined with pretty flowers and up the porch steps. Once inside the little blue house, we were introduced to Mrs. Moseley's best friend and constant companion, Herman the beagle, an animal shelter rescue.

We found Mrs. Moseley's art to be similar to that of the legendary Grandma Moses, yet, as her critics have remarked, Mrs. Moseley offers something extra—a sense of humor. Each painting has a quirky title: *Life has so many Angles, Git up to Snuff, You've Time Enough,* or *Life is so Daily.* There is a story behind each painting, and this unique lady has accumulated many stories in her lifetime of ninety-four years.

After a series of unfortunate trials, losing her father to suicide, nursing her mother through a long siege of Alzheimer's, and then watching her beloved husband pass away, she chose to go on with life and make the most of every day. Her advice for achieving a long, satisfying life: "Find a reason for getting up every morning, something that takes your mind off yourself, then get up every day and do it." She also believes there is enormous talent in older people that often goes undiscovered.

Mrs. Moseley is a self-taught artist who began painting in her sixties during a stressful time in her life. "I just picked up a cheap set of paints and began," she said. "I didn't even know I could do it." Her work has achieved acclaim from art critics, art educators, and art collectors and has appeared in shows and museum exhibits throughout the South.

When I asked her why she chose to live in Bay St. Louis, she said she had received five invitations (all for the same weekend) to show her art. Not knowing which to choose, she asked someone to pick an envelope randomly. The lucky draw was Bay St. Louis, Mississippi. "The minute I drove across the bridge and saw the ocean gently lapping against the sand," remarked Mrs. Moseley, "I liked what I saw." Being Presbyterian, she believes in predestination. Thus, the lady artist and the rescued beagle living together in the blue cottage were preordained by the Lord.

As Herman watched, my husband and I purchased an art print: *The House is Blue but the Old Lady Ain't;* a picture of the blue house, with the lady dancing out front. Herman stands beside Mrs. Moseley while an angel is watching from above.

I just described a memory from years ago. Later, Hurricane Katrina hit Bay St. Louis with a vengeance, destroying the historical Bed and Breakfast we had visited, and perhaps it demolished the little blue house. However, Mrs. Moseley passed before the event of Katrina. Her story is not merely about Folk Art. It is about the art of Living—taking what life brings and giving back with what one has to offer the world.

A SENSE OF PURPOSE

It is not enough to have lived. We should be determined to live for something.

—Dr. Leo Buscaglia

In *Keep Sharp,* Dr. Sanjay Gupta writes of the importance of having a sense of purpose at every age. He tells the story of his mother who was forced to flee an area of the world that is now Pakistan, at the age of five. "It was during the time of the bloody Indian subcontinent partition," writes Dr. Gupta. "Along with her family, my mother joined one of the largest human migrations in history. After arriving in India, she lived as a refugee for the next several years, struggling to survive."

Dr. Gupta emphasizes that people in those refugee camps didn't have the luxury of hopes, dreams, and aspirations. Nevertheless, Dr. Gupta's grandmother, a woman who had completed only the fourth grade, was determined that her daughter would get an education. She assured her daughter that someday she would become someone who mattered. "My mom completed engineering college in India and made history as the first female engineer there. After reading a biography of Henry Ford, my mom dreamed of working for the company that he had built. My grandparents took their life savings to send my mom to the United States in 1965. At age twenty-four, she became the first woman hired as an engineer at Ford Motor Company."

Dr. Gupta says there is no shortage of ways to stay engaged and maintain a sense of purpose. He tells us, "You don't have to keep a regular job. You can enroll in a class to learn something new, volunteer, teach, renew your library card, work on your hobbies, be a good friend to your neighbors, or turn your garden into a sanctuary."

FINDING THE MUSE AT SIXTY

If there is a book you really want to read but it hasn't been written yet, then you must write it.

—Toni Morrison

Sitting in church on a Sunday morning, I heard the pastor ask, "What would you attempt to do if you knew you would not fail?" He gave instructions: "Search your heart for the answer, and then pray and ask God to help you accomplish His plans for your life."

Immediately, I knew the answer: If I could do anything, I would become a writer. But that was impossible. Weren't writers born with the gift? Didn't all writers have college degrees and sharp minds? Didn't they simply sit down every day, listen to the whispers of their muses and create? Becoming a writer seemed very unlikely for me—I didn't even have a muse.

Nevertheless, I prayed a silent prayer, left the church, and thought little of it. Several weeks later, I was indulging in my favorite pastime— browsing in Books-a-Million, when I came across a large book jutting out from the shelf. As I lifted it out and leafed through the pages, I stopped at these words: "Anyone can write." I had absentmindedly wandered into the Craft of Writing section. Among all those books was a message for me—an answer to my prayer.

Soon, I found the courage to register for classes at the local community college. In my <u>first </u>creative writing class, my classmates were sporting tattoos, multiple piercings, and tongue baubles. They wrote stories of rape and incest and coming out in the gay world. As I sat and listened to their tales, I realized that a grandmother like me, approaching her sixtieth year in the world, had valuable words to share with them.

In a literature class, I read the works of Greek writers and learned that they began their tales by calling on their gods for help. I didn't believe in their muses, but I began to see it so clearly—I did have a

Muse. He is the author of the Bible, the One who put the desire to write in my heart.

WHY DIDN'T SOMEBODY DO SOMETHING?

After visiting the Holocaust Museum, an eleven-year-old girl walked out and exclaimed, "Why didn't somebody do something?" In our world today, with tragedy and horror abounding, will our great grandchildren one day exclaim, "Why didn't somebody do something?"

No matter how old you are, no matter how infirmed, there is something you can do for the future of your children and grandchildren, and for your country. No matter how overwhelmed you feel, even if you have no idea how God can use you in this world, there is one powerful thing you can do. He will use your daily, focused prayers to bring good things into existence and to change our world.

A marvelous example of this is an event in 1949, in the Scottish Islands. Two women, one of them eighty-four years old and the other eighty-two and blind, were greatly burdened because of the appalling state of their parish. They were especially grieved that young people did not know God and were staying away from church. Both women decided to spend extra time in prayer twice a week. They began praying at ten o'clock on Tuesday and Friday evenings and remained in prayer until three or four o'clock in the morning. This went on for months, and then one night, one of the sisters had a vision where her church was crowded with young people. She then sent for the parish minister and told him of her vision. The minister organized a prayer meeting with seven men praying long hours twice a week. As a result of these prayers, a great revival enveloped the island and continued for three years. People were saved, lives were changed, and the atmosphere of the whole island was transformed.

Perhaps our world is waiting for us to do something. As God's children, we have assignments even in our older years. I agree with the Quaker minister, Elizabeth Fry, who said, "If you will do what you can do, God will do what you cannot do. Doors will open, a way will be made and creative ideas will come. Inspire others, each person doing a little, together we can make a big difference."

HOW DID I GET SO OLD?

In Andy Andrews' book, *The Noticer,* the angel-like character Jones discusses age with a very weary lady. The lady explained that her life was over, she had outlived her usefulness, and it was time for her to go. She says, "I am an old woman wishing merely to live out my days without being in the way of those who still have much to do." Not willing to accept her negativity, Jones said, "Woo wee! And aren't we glad everybody doesn't feel that way! The world would surely have missed out on some grand achievements." With this, he begins a list of people who accomplished important things in their senior years:

Colonel Sanders, at age sixty-five, took a family recipe and began franchising fried chicken. Benjamin Franklin invented the bifocals when he was seventy-eight. After serving time in prison, Nelson Mandela, was inaugurated President of South Africa at the age of seventy-five. Igor Stravinsky was still performing concerts at eighty-seven. When he was seventy-two, Michelangelo began his work on one of the world's greatest treasures, St Peter's Basilica.

Jones encourages, "Just seek to make a tiny difference in someone's life." He reminds us that our time on earth is a gift to be used wisely: "Don't squander your words or your thoughts. Consider that the simplest actions you take matter beyond measure. They matter forever."

Chapter Six

Hopes and Dreams

It's always been my belief that you never get too old to dream. I often say that I wake up with a new dream every day. Dreaming is easy. Making them come true is the hard part. A wish and a dream are not the same. You can sit around and wish all day about wanting this and wanting that. But that's not gonna get you anywhere if you don't dream up a plan and act on it. You have to put legs, arms, feet, hands, and wings on them... A dream is a dream, and it can come true at any age.

–Dolly Parton

POSSIBLE DREAMS

When a dream in your heart is one that God planted there, a strange happiness flows into us. At that moment all of the spiritual resources of the universe are released to help us. Our praying is then at one with the will of God and becomes a channel for the Creator.

—Catherine Marshall

Motivational speaker John Maxwell says, "The real difference between a dream and wishful thinking is what you do day to day." He tells us to write out a clear description of the dream, including its main features or objectives. Next, write out a plan for achieving the dream.

Maxwell gives advises:

- Do something. Do anything if you are a naturally sedentary person or someone who is discouraged.
- Do something that relates to your dream and will advance you toward your dream today.
- Do something every day that relates to your dream. If you do the right things day after day, you will make progress and will eventually achieve what you set out to do.

Maxwell suggests that we consider these questions: Have I made significant changes to my priorities and work habits to put my plan into action? Have I considered what I am willing to trade to achieve my dream? Am I willing to do something every day—even if it's very small to move closer to my dreams? Will people other than myself benefit from my realized dream?

Bruce Wilkinson, in his book *You Were Born for This,* says, "Our dream was never meant to be just a remote possibility for us but a completed achievement. God plans for each of us to accomplish our dream."

Wilkinson instructs:

- Our dream was invented by God, not us.
- Our dream is why God formed us and explains who we are and why we are here.
- Our dream was never meant to be optional. It is an indispensable part of God's dream for this time and place.

Mark Twain said: "The secret of getting ahead is getting started. The secret of getting started is breaking your complex, overwhelming tasks into small manageable tasks, and then starting on the first one."

WRITING A GOOD STORY

The thief does not come except to steal, and to kill, and to destroy. I have come that they may have life, and that they may have it more abundantly.

—John 10:10

In *A Million Miles in a Thousand Years,* Donald Miller writes: "We live in a world where bad stories are told, stories that teach us life doesn't mean anything and that humanity has no great purpose. It's a good calling, then, to speak a better story."

Miller believes we can edit our lives into great stories by taking responsibility to find the right answers to problems and to fulfill the tasks which life constantly offers each of us. His personal story goes from sleeping all day to riding his bike across America, from wasting his money to founding a non-profit Mentoring program. We see Donald Miller replacing a useless plot with meaningful narrative.

Instead of plotting his own life, Miller has learned that God knows the story as it should be told, and will guide him in the right direction. He says, "There is a knowing I feel that guides me toward being a better character. I believe there is a Writer outside ourselves, plotting a better story for us, interacting with us, and whispering a better story into our consciousness." He believes it is always better to obey the whispering writer, the One who knows the better story, even though, the Writer often instructs us to put something into the script that we do not feel comfortable with.

Miller believes that humans naturally seek comfort and stability and that without an inciting incident that disrupts their comfort, they won't enter into God's story. "The character has to jump into the story," says

Miller, "into the discomfort and the fear, otherwise, the story will never happen." When we are pushed out of our comfort zone, fear can stop us. Yet, we are told countless times in the Bible, "Do not Fear." Miller warns, "Don't let fear boss you around."

Miller speaks of a "force" in the world that doesn't want us to live good stories. He says, "It doesn't want us to face our issues, to face our fear and bring something beautiful into the world." This force is the "thief" spoken of in John 10:10. When the enemy shows up, we must look fear in the face with courage. "After all," says Miller, "If a story doesn't have negative turns, it's not an interesting story. A protagonist who understands this idea lives a better story. He doesn't give up when he encounters a setback because he knows that every story has both positive and negative turns."

Miller believes that God is saying to each of us, "Write a good story, take somebody with you, and let Me Help you."

THE CLIMB

Every choice will give you the chance to go lower, to stay the same, or to go higher. Choose the higher path, even if it's harder, take the higher step. Let each of your steps be higher than the step before it. You will end up walking the mountain heights.

–Jonathan Cahn

My nighttime dreams rarely make any sense at all. However, I believe I once dreamed a God-given dream. In this dream, I was climbing what seemed to be a mountain, but it was more like a giant tree with short limbs jutting out from the trunk. Midway of the climb, the fear of falling gripped me like a bone-crushing vice. I dared not look down or I was sure to fall. I knew the summit I was struggling to reach was not heaven. Rather, it was something or some things I was to accomplish with my life before reaching heaven. Paralyzed with fear, I had stopped halfway when a strange thing happened. A small child (my little granddaughter Molly) scampered up past me, reached the top, and disappeared. I knew then if a little child could go there so easily, I must continue the climb.

I reached up to the limb above me and hoisted myself up closer to the next limb. I reached again, grasping the higher limb with all my strength, and then I heard a sickening crack. The limb holding all my weight was breaking in two Expecting to fall to the ground, I fell back instead. I fell into strong arms that held me in place.

When I woke from the dream, I knew the meaning: The Lord wanted me to continue climbing despite my fear, trusting His arms to hold me. When I asked about the child who so easily reached the summit, I heard the words: "It is the faith of a little child that will take you up."

The mountains we are to climb will look scary. When we begin our upward climb, there is always a chance of falling and completely failing. I was afraid of falling, afraid of failure. But if God has ordained the climb, He will either hold me in place, or should I fall, He will pick me up, dust me off, and send me climbing again. I must keep moving up.

"It is the Lord who directs your life, for each step you take is ordained by God to bring you closer to your destiny"
(Proverbs 20:24, Passion Bible).

THE PATH BEFORE YOU

Set your gaze on the path before you with fixed purpose, looking straight ahead.

— Proverbs 4:25

Watch where you are going! Stick to the path of truth, and the road will be safe and smooth before you. Don't allow yourself to be sidetracked for even a moment or take the detour that leads to darkness.

– Proverbs 4:26-27

I treasure the tattered, yellow pages of my Og Mandino books. They contain priceless information on how to live life. In *The Greatest Salesman in the World*, read by more than nine million people, I find the Ten Vows of Success:

First vow: *"I was born to succeed, not to fail."* I was formed in the image of God. There is nothing I cannot achieve if I try.

Second: *Never again will I greet the dawn without a map.* I need a plan for each day; no matter how small, daily goals bring me closer to my destiny.

Third: *Always will I bathe my days in the golden glow of enthusiasm.* Enthusiasm in all I do will become, with hard work, a habit. Should I stumble now and then, I will pick myself up and go on with my life.

Fourth: *Never again will I be disagreeable to a living soul.* If I frown, I will meet a frown in return. If I shout in anger, angry voices will respond.

Fifth: *Always will I seek the seed of triumph in every adversity.* If I turn to God, any time of adversity can be transformed into a triumphant turning point in my life.

Sixth: *Never again will I perform my task at less than my best.* I will remain at my task, just a little longer, and let that extra effort be an investment in my tomorrow.

Seventh: *Always will I throw my whole self into the task at hand.* I will leave my traces. The world will know I've been there.

Eighth: *Never again will I wait and hope for opportunity to embrace me.* The opportunity knocks at no door. I must knock, often and loud.

Ninth: *Always will I examine, each night, my deeds of the fading day.* What infirmity have I mastered today? What passion opposed? What temptation resisted? What virtue acquired?

Tenth: *Always will I maintain contact, through prayer with my Creator.* The greatest talent God has bestowed upon me is the power to pray. In the morning, prayer will open for me the treasures of God's blessings. And in the evening, it is the key that places me under His protection. Without prayer, I can do little; with it all things are possible.

GOD KNOWS ALL ABOUT ME

Lord, you know everything there is to know about me.
You perceive every movement of my heart and soul,
And you understand my every thought before it even enters my mind.
You are so intimately aware of me, Lord.
You read my heart like an open book and you
know all the words I am about to speak
Before I even start a sentence! You know every step I
will take before my journey even begins.
You've gone into my future to prepare the way,
And in kindness you follow behind me to spare
me from the harm of my past.
With your hand of love upon my life, you impart a blessing to me.
This is just too wonderful, deep and incomprehensible!
Your understanding of me brings me wonder and strength.
Where could I go from your spirit? Where
could I run and hide from your face?
Oh yes, you shaped me first inside, then out:
You formed me in my mother's womb.
I thank You, High God—You are breathtaking!
Body and soul, I am marvelously made!
I worship in adoration—what a creation!
You know me inside and out, You know every bone in my body;
You know exactly how I was made, bit by bit,
How I was sculpted from nothing to something.
Like an open book, you watched me grow from conception to birth;
All the stages of my life were spread out before you,
The days of my life all prepared before I'd even lived one day....
God, I invite your searching gaze into my heart.
examine me through and through.
Find out anything that may be hidden within me.
Put me to the test and sift through all my anxious cares.

See if there is any path of pain I'm walking on, and lead me back to your Glorious, everlasting ways—the path that brings me back to you.
—Psalm 139 Passion Bible

I believe that when God knit me together in my mother's womb, His Spirit hovered over me with a plan for my life. He "Formed my inner-most being." He wrote His best plans for me in His book and gave me everything I would need to accomplish my God-given destiny. I am responsible for pursuing the life that He has identified as best and doing the work necessary for its accomplishment. Assignments for each of Gods children are individual and unique. Ephesians 2:10, in the Passion Bible reads: "We have become His poetry, a re-created people who will fulfill the destiny He has given each of us, for we are joined to Jesus, the anointed One. Even before we were born, God planned in advance our destiny and the good works we would do to fulfill it."

Holocaust survivor Eli Wiesel wrote: "When you die and go to meet your Maker, you're not going to be asked why you didn't become a doctor or find a cure for cancer. All you're going to be asked is, 'Why didn't you become you? Why didn't you become all that you are?'"

In Max Lucado's book, *Glory Days,* he writes, "No one else has your 'you-ness.' No one else in history has your unique history. No one else in God's great design has your blend of personality and ability. When God made you, the angels stood in awe and declared, 'We've never seen one like that before.' And they never will again. Consequently, you can do something no one else can do in a fashion no one else can."

Assignments for each of God's children are individual and unique. "Each person is given something to do that shows who God is" (Ephesians 5:17 Message Bible).

However, along the path toward our ultimate destiny, we will have many commitments, obligations that take our time. In *Magnolia Journal Magazine,* Joanna Gaines says, "Daily obligations come with laundry that needs folding, bills waiting to be paid, and bodies that need to be fed. We understand that life is all about the balance of things. And that without that balance, there'd be no tension to move us forward. It's often with the consistent and daily return to our commitments that our future takes shape." Gaines tells us that it is these daily actions that shape our place in the world, and she says, "We must remember that "purpose" isn't found in one sweeping gesture but in the daily forging of a devoted life. So that we can trust that our commitments aren't what hold us back, but are the very things holding us up."

Michelle Sassa writes, in *Magnolia Journal Magazine:* "Some of us find fulfillment in raising a family, pursuing a passion, making the world a better place." She asks the questions, "What is it that pulls you out of bed each morning, thinking, Let's do this? What are you grateful for as you lay back down and reflect on your day?" Sassa advises: "Recognizing the value in everyday toils can bring clarity that helps us decide where to devote our hearts and our time. Our daily practices and efforts help us keep the promises we've made—to others and to ourselves. As you piece your way through the puzzle, keep an eye on the big picture."

WALK INTO YOUR DESTINY

In the book of Joshua, we see that God had a plan for His Hebrew Children to reach the Promised Land—their ultimate destiny. In preparation for the journey, God would open the Jordan River and break down the Walls of Jericho—He would even cause the sun to stand still.

> "The Lord spoke to Joshua saying, 'Therefore, arise, go over the Jordon, you and all the people, to the land which I am giving them. Every place that the sole of your foot will tread upon I am giving you. I will be with you. I will not leave you or forsake you. Only be strong and very courageous, that you may observe to do according to the law. This book of the law will not depart from your mouth, but you shall meditate on it day and night that you may observe to do according to

all that is written in it. For then you will make your way
prosperous, and then you will have good success. Have
I not commanded you? Be strong and of good courage;
do not be afraid, nor dismayed, for the Lord God is
with you wherever you go'" (Joshua 1:1-8).

Remember that your mission is accomplished as you walk within
God's will. Author Diane Noble explains: "Each person's relationship
with God is individual, personal. He rarely works exactly the same way
twice. The shoes He gives will fit you exactly, the signposts will seem
written just for you, and the joy will spur you on."

I am thankful that each of us has a place in God's great big picture.
Alone we are odd-shaped, peculiar, and undeveloped. He made us to
complement others, to join in beside other shapes in the puzzle. Some
pieces of the Puzzle will stand out and loom larger than others. Some
of us will be tiny supporters of the larger ones, but we are all necessary
parts of God's "Big Picture."

"I leave my destiny and its timing in Your Hands, Lord
God. Your pleasant path leads me to pleasant places.
I'm overwhelmed with the privileges that come with
following you, for You have given me the best! Your
whispers in the night give me wisdom showing me what
to do next. I experience Your wrap-around presence
every moment."

—Psalm 16 –Passion Bible

Notes

CHAPTER ONE

Thomas Kinkade, *Lightposts for Living,* New York, N.Y., Warner Books, 1999.

Chris Gardner, *The Pursuit of Happiness.* New York N.Y., Harper Collins, 2006

Maxwell King, *The Good Neighbor,* New York, N.Y., Abrams Press 2018.

Sandy Dangler, *Susanna Wesley,* Chicago, Il., Moody Press, 1987.

CHAPTER TWO

Corrie Ten Boom, *Tramp for the Lord, 1974.*

Frank Peretti, *Wounded Spirit,* Nashville, Tn, Word Publishers, 2000.

Elizabeth Smart, *My Story,* New York, N.Y., St. Martian's Press, 2013.

Tyler Perry, *Higher is Waiting,* New York, Spiegel & Grau, Random House, 2017.

J.D. Vance, *Hillbilly Elegy,* New York, N.Y., Harper Collins, 2010

Ben Carson, *Gifted Hands,* Grand Rapids, Michigan, Zondervan, 2010

Laura Hillenbrand, *Unbroken, New York, N.Y.,* Random House, 2010.

Chapter Three

Jeffrey Rosensweig, *Age Smart,* Saddle River, New Jersey, Prentice Hall, 2006.

Sanjay Gupta, *Keep Sharp,* New York, N.Y., Simon & Schuster, 2021.

Andy Andrews, *The Final Summit,* Nashville, Tn. Thomas Nelson, 2010.

Noel B. Gerson, *Harriet Beecher Stowe,* New York, N.Y., Praeger Publishers, 1976.

Chapter Four

Max Lucado, *Glory Days,* Nashville, Tn. Thomas Nelson, 2015.

Louis L'Amour, *The Education of a Wandering Man,* New York, Bantam Books, 1989.

Chapter Five

Andy Andrews, *The Noticer,* Nashville, Tennessee, Thomas Nelson, *2009.*

Ben Carson, *Gifted Hands.* Grand Rapids, Michigan, Zondervan, 1990.

Andy Andrews, *The Little Things.* Nashville Tennessee, Thomas Nelson, 2017

Chapter Six

John C. Maxwell, *Put Your Dream to the Test,* Nashville, Tennessee, Thomas Nelson, 2009.

Bruce Wilkinson, *You* Were *Born for This,* Colorado Springs, Colorado, Multnomah Books, 2009.

Donald Miller, Donald, *A Million Miles in a Thousand Years,* Nashville, Tennessee, Thomas Nelson, 2009.

Andy Andrews, *The Final Summit,* Nashville, Tn., Thomas Nelson, 2010. (Author's note on Churchill)

Chip and Joanna Gaines, *The Magnolia Story,* Nashville, Tn. Thomas Nelson, 2016

Og Mandino, *The Greatest Salesman in the World Part 11.* Bantam Books, New York, N.Y. 1988.